Martina Funder
Die VerTonung der Welt
The World Composed in Clay

VERLAG FÜR MODERNE KUNST

Martina Funder
Die VerTonung der Welt
The World Composed in Clay

Mit Texten von With texts by

Rainald Franz, Renée Gadsden, Hartwig Knack und and Anna Lorenz

Inhalt Contents

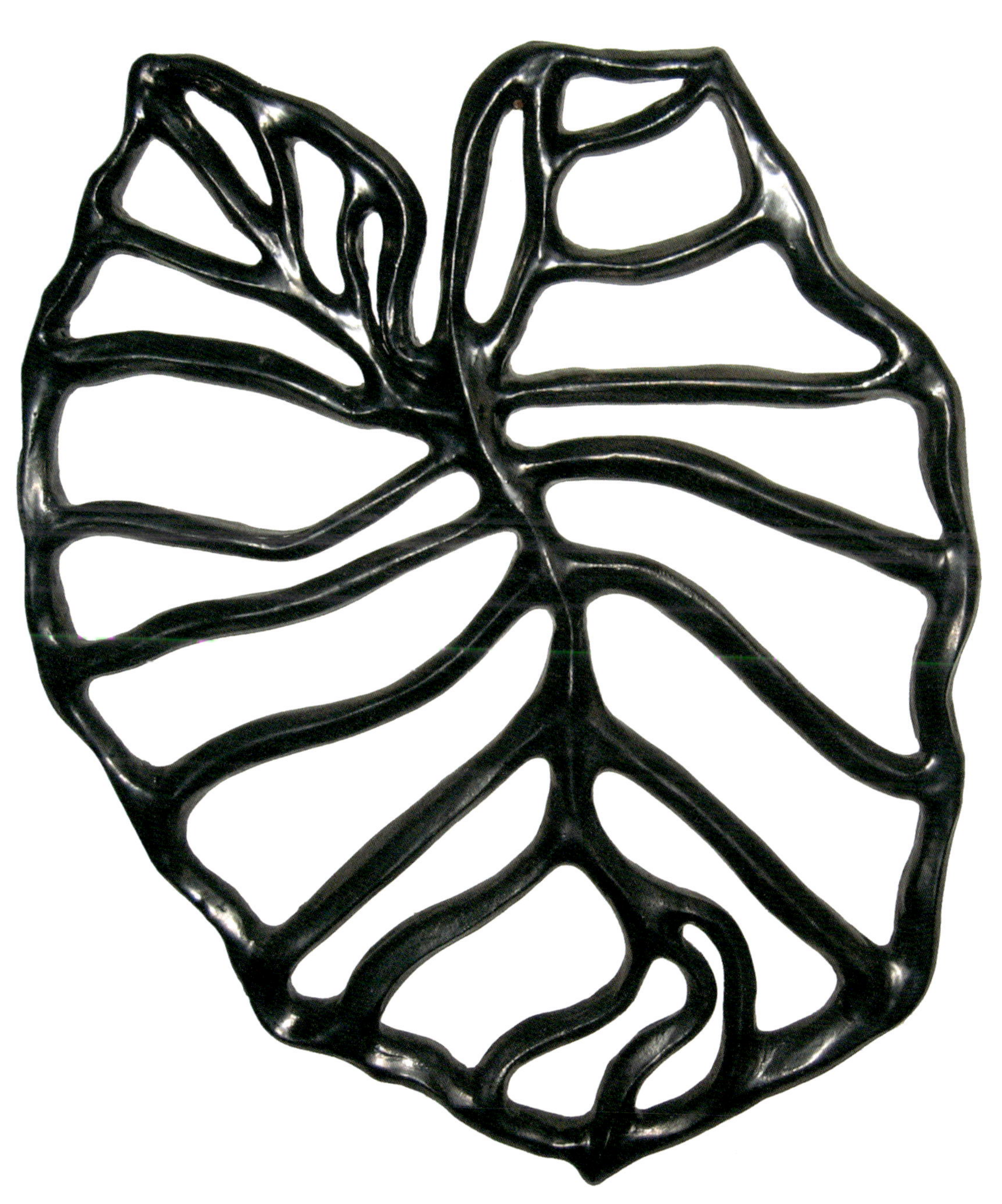

Rainald Franz

Die VerTonung der Welt

Martina Funders Arbeit mit und an der Keramik

Die Keramikerin Martina Funder hat sich dem Material Ton, das der Erde am Nächsten ist, ja, aus ihr entsteht, über einen „Umweg" angenähert. Unter „Umweg" versteht sie ihre Maleereiausbildung an der Akademie der bildenden Künste und auch noch die Jahre danach, in denen sie viel gemalt und gezeichnet hat. Ihren ersten eigenen Brennofen konnte sie sich durch Malerei finanzieren. Es hat sich durch Zeichnen und Malen eine eigene Sicht auf die Dinge der Welt und daher eine eigene Umgangsweise mit dem Ton ergeben, den sie sich seit ihrem Diplom an der Hochschule für künstlerische und industrielle Gestaltung Linz, Meisterklasse für Keramik, auf mannigfache Weise zu eigen gemacht.

Bereits in Johann Joachim Winckelmanns *Geschichte der Kunst des Alterthums* (1764) finden wir die Annahme einer historisch ersten Kunst und eines bestimmten Materials, in dem zum ersten Mal Gegenstände der bildenden Kunst geschaffen wurden. Winckelmann schreibt von der Materie, in welcher die Bildhauerei ihre Werke herausgearbeitet hat. Diese ist für ihn der Ton, „mit dem die Kunst anfing. Den Ton, als die erste Materie der Kunst, deuten selbst die alten Sprachen an."

Und Gottfried Semper schreibt in seiner Vorrede zur Keramik im Hauptwerk *Der Stil in den technischen und tektonischen Künsten oder praktische Ästhetik* (1879): „Man zeige die Töpfe, die ein volk hervorbrachte und es läßt sich im allgemeinen sagen, welcher art es war und auf welcher stufe der bildung es sich befand. Nicht nur den Töpfen wohnt die offenbarungskraft inne, möchte man hinzufügen. Jeder gebrauchsgegenstand kann uns von sitten, dem charakter eines volkes erzählen. Aber die produkte der keramik besitzen diese Eigenschaft am sinnfälligsten."

Es soll hier nicht behauptet werden, dass diese Zitate und Haltungen Martina Funders Weg in die Keramik bestimmt haben. Betrachtet man aber ihre künstlerische Entwicklung als Keramikerin entlang ihrer Arbeiten, dann ergeben sich Parallelen. Martina Funders Werke drängen zu einer Ausschöpfung des „Möglichkeitssystems" Ton, indem sie das Material mit tektonischen, ikonografischen, politischen, multikulturellen Inhalten aufladen, die in ihnen zur Form finden.

Auszugehen ist von einer familiären Prägung durch die Bezüge zu einer der ältesten in Wien ansässigen Hafnerdynastien, die sich auch bis heute in der ständigen Beschäftigung Martina Funders mit dem Kachelofenentwurf und -bau niederschlägt. Das Ofensetzen aus Ton, ein struktiver, fast architektonischer Prozess, führt zu autonomen Entitäten.

In Martina Funders Arbeiten der letzten zehn Jahre konstatiert man eine Dominanz des Organischen und Struktiven in den Formen. Naturformen, vom Bergmassiv en miniature *(Berg der Steinböcke,* 2015) über Ast- und Blattformen *(Löwenzahnblatt,* 2003, *Cut 1* und *Cut 2,* 2010, *Blatt und sein Gerippe,* 2010) bis zur Schneedecke *(Schneedecke von Zhovkva,* 2016), stehen für die Auseinandersetzung mit den *Kunstformen der Natur,* wie sie der Biologe Ernst Haeckel 1904 als Lithographien mit durchschlagender Wirkung auf die moderne Kunst publizierte. Martina Funder nähert sich den Formen in ihrer Wahrnehmung, bereitet vor und begleitet mit Bleistiftzeichnungen in Umrissen. Das von Wind und Wetter Geformte wird so als kunstvoll identifiziert. Organisch gewachsen ist hier die in Ton festgehaltene Form, die weiter der Veränderung ausgesetzt ist, quasi eine Momentaufnahme des Massiven wie des Fragilen.

Dazu treten Schöpfungen, die das Interesse der Künstlerin an der Qualität des Struktiven erkennen lassen, sei es in vom Menschen herbeigeführter Form, also in allen Formen der Architektur *(Inkamauer, Inkamatratze,* 2014) bis zu gerüsthaften Konstruktionen in Ton *(Modul 1-2-3,* 2007, *die schwarze Mauer,* 2009). Archaische Strukturen, die den Betrachter den Vergleich mit Werken Franz Josef Altenburgs ziehen lassen.

Im Organischen wie im Struktiven scheint Martina Funder auf der Suche nach der Urform zu sein, der künstlerisch kreative Prozess der Recherche, der zur Formfindung führt, wird durch Reisen und Naturbeobachtung angeregt. Muster und Oberflächengestaltung liest die Künstlerin als Zeichen, die in Arbeiten wie *die Gestreiften* (2009) oder *Pongal* (2009) dem haptischen Material Ton entsprechend aus der Fläche ins Dreidimensionale treten.

Dieser erkennbaren Systematisierung, dem ordnenden Impetus in Martina

Holzscheit
1991
gebrannter und glasierter Ton
19 x 60 x 11 cm

wooden log
1991
fired and glazed clay
19 x 60 x 11 cm

Funders Werk entspricht auch die rezente Schöpfung des *rosa Regals* (2015). Darin geht sie über das angestammte Material Ton hinaus in Richtung Installation, im aus Metall und rosa Acrylglas errichteten Ordnungssystem erhalten die Tonarbeiten jedoch einen neuen, zusätzlichen Aspekt, der an Naturalienkabinette und Kunstkammern erinnert. Das *rosa Regal* ist nicht diaphan und daher auch nicht ausschließlich Lager-, sondern auch Umgestaltungsort, das dem Dialog der Tonarbeiten einen neuen Aspekt gibt.

Ihr keramischer Beitrag zur Ausstellung 2016 im Kaiserhaus Baden wiederum führt eine Behandlung des Tons als Mittel naturähnlicher Nachahmung vor. Äpfel und Birnen, ganz und angebissen, werden naturalistisch wiedergegeben, wie historische Wachsnachformungen in Naturkundemuseen, aber durch die Verweigerung der veristischen Bemalung und Glasur werden sie wiederum als Kunstform definiert.

Martina Funders Arbeiten sichern dem Ton als Kunstmedium Ausdruckskraft jenseits banaler Nachahmung. Die VerTonung der Welt setzt sich in ihrem selbst gewählten System der Erkenntnis mit für den Betrachter überraschenden Ergebnissen immer weiter fort, ohne universalistische Ansprüche zu stellen. Ihre Arbeiten sind Angebote zur Weltwahrnehmung an den Betrachter, die zum Dialog anregen.

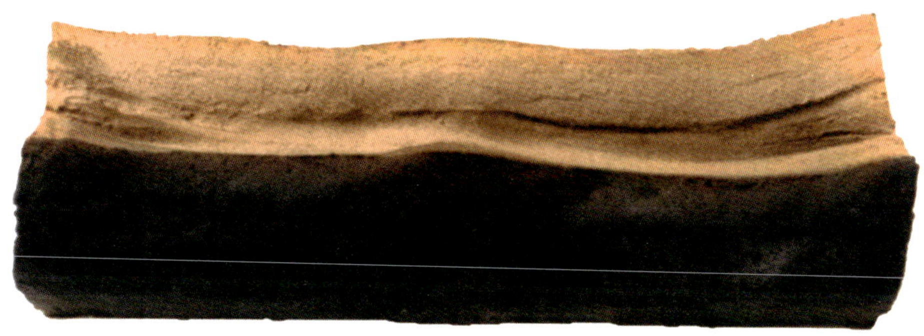

Rainald Franz

The World Composed in Clay

Martina Funder's work on and with ceramics

Ceramics artist Martina Funder has approached the medium of clay, which is closest in composition to that of the earth, and indeed has its origins in the earth, via a "detour." She sees this "detour" to be her study of painting at the Academy of Fine Arts and also the years which followed her studies, during which she did a great deal of drawing and painting. Through her painting, she financed her very first kiln. Drawing and painting have profoundly influenced the way the artist views the world, and thus also imparted her with a unique approach to her work with clay, an approach which she has continued to hone and make her own in many-faceted ways since completing the master class in ceramics and earning her diploma from the Academy of Art and Industrial Design in Linz.

Already in Johann Joachim Winckelmann's *History of the Art of Antiquity* (1764) we find the assumption of a historical origin of art and a particular material from which, for the first time, objects of visual arts were created. Winckelmann writes of the material in which sculpture has worked out its craft. For him, this is clay, "with which art first began. Even the ancient languages point to clay as the first material of art."

And Gottfried Semper writes in his preface to ceramics in his work, *The Style in the Technical and Tectonic Arts; or, Practical Aesthetics* (1879): "Examine the pottery which a folk or society created, and one can generally determine the type of people and their level of education. Not only the pots possess an inherent revelational power, one might add; any object of use can tell us about the morals, the character of a people. But the products of ceramics possess this characteristic most strikingly."

This is not to say that these quotes and discussions have determined Martina Funder's path into ceramics and pottery. However, considerations of her artistic development as a ceramicist viewed alongside her work beg such parallels. Martina Funder urges the realization of clay's full potentiality by charging the material with tectonic, iconographic, political, multicultural content which find expressional form in her pieces.

The point of departure is from a family background with direct references to one of the oldest Viennese potter dynasties, which also is reflected in Funder's constant preoccupation with kiln design and construction. Building kilns from clay, a structural, almost architectural process, results in autonomous entities.

The forms found in Martina Funder's work from the last decade display a predominance of the organic and the structural. Natural forms, a mountain massif in miniature *(Berg der Steinböcke [mountain of ibexes]*, 2015) as well as branch and leaf shapes *(Löwenzahnblatt [dandelion leaf]*, 2003; *cut 1 and cut 2*, 2010; *Blatt und sein Gerippe [leaf and its skeleton]*, 2010), snow cover *(Schneedecke von Zhovkva [snow cover in Zhovkva]*, 2016), all represent the confrontation with the art forms of nature, as published in the eponymous lithograph works of the biologist Ernst Haeckel in 1904, which had a resounding effect on modern art. Martina Funder approaches forms with her own unique perception, prepares and accompanies with pencil drawings in outline. Her work identifies the artistic aspects of natural forms which wind and weather have shaped. Organically grown forms are captured in clay, forms which will be subjected to further change, a virtual snapshot of the massive and the fragile.

Additionally, there are creations which reveal the ceramicist's interest in the quality of the structural element, either induced in man-made form, that is, in all forms of architecture *(Inkamauer, Inkamatratze [Inca wall, Inca mattress]*, 2014), to scaffold-like constructions in clay *(Modul [module] 1-2-3*, 2007; *die schwarze Mauer [the black wall]*, 2009), archaic structures that allow the viewer to make a comparison with the works of Franz Josef Altenburg.

In the organic as in the structural, Martina Funder seems to be looking for the primeval form, the artistic creative process of research, leading to the form-finding process and inspired by travel and the observation of nature.

The artist interprets patterns and surface design as signs which, in keeping with the haptic material of clay, step from the surface into the three-dimensional in works such as *die Gestreiften (the striped)*, 2009, or *Pongal*, 2009.

die schwarze Mauer
2009
gebrannter und glasierter Ton
42 x 90 x 20 cm

the black wall
2009
fired and glazed clay
42 x 90 x 20 cm

This recognizable systematization, the ordering and organizational impetus in Martina Funder's work, also corresponds to the recent creation of the *rosa Regal* (pink cabinet), 2015. In this work, she goes beyond the inherent aspects of clay to the genre of installation; in the storage system built of metal and pink acrylic, clay gains a new, supplementary aspect, reminiscent of natural history cabinets and cabinets of art and curios. The *rosa Regal* is not diaphanous and therefore not only an object of storage, but also place of transformation that gives new insight to the dialogue of pottery.

Funder's ceramic contribution to the exhibition in 2016 in the Kaiserhaus (imperial summer residence) in Baden results in a treatment of clay as a means of simulating and imitating nature. Apples and pears, whole and partly eaten, are naturalistically rendered, much like historical wax copies in natural history museums; but by refusing to veristically paint and glaze them, she defines them as an art form.

Martina Funder's work secures the expressiveness of clay as an art medium beyond banal imitation. The "clay setting" of the world continues in its self-imposed system of recognition with surprising twists and turns for the viewer, without making universalist claims. Her works encourage dialogue and are offers to the viewer to perceive the world afresh.

Kokons Verwandlung
1989
gebrannter und glasierter Ton
6 x 70 x 7 cm

metamorphosis of a cocoon
1989
fired and glazed clay
6 x 70 x 7 cm

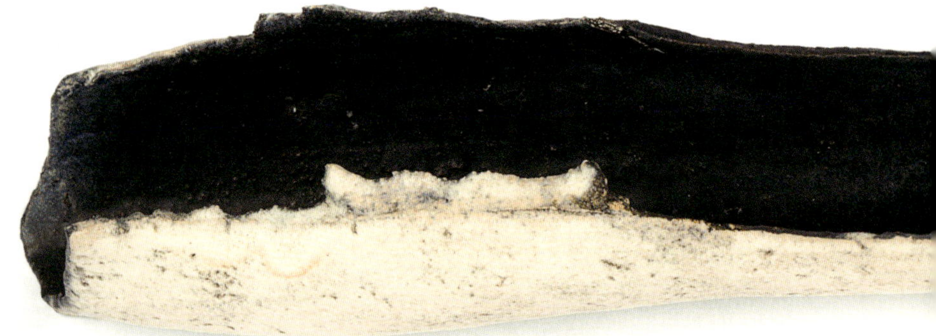

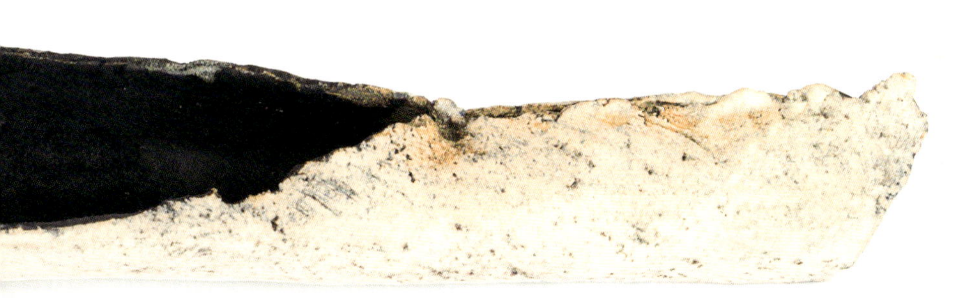

Sturmäste
1991
4 Stück, gebrannter Ton
längstes Stück 70 cm

storm branches
1991
4 pieces, fired clay
longest piece 70 cm

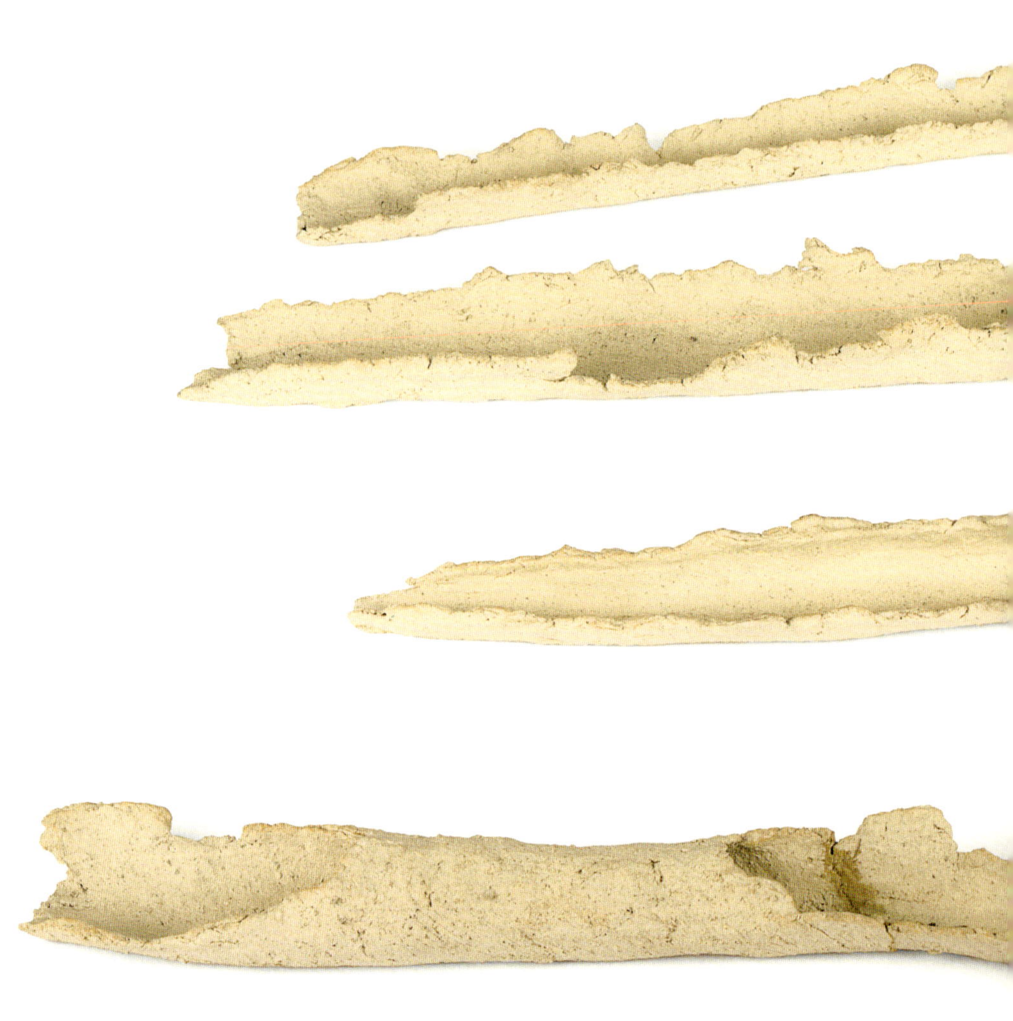

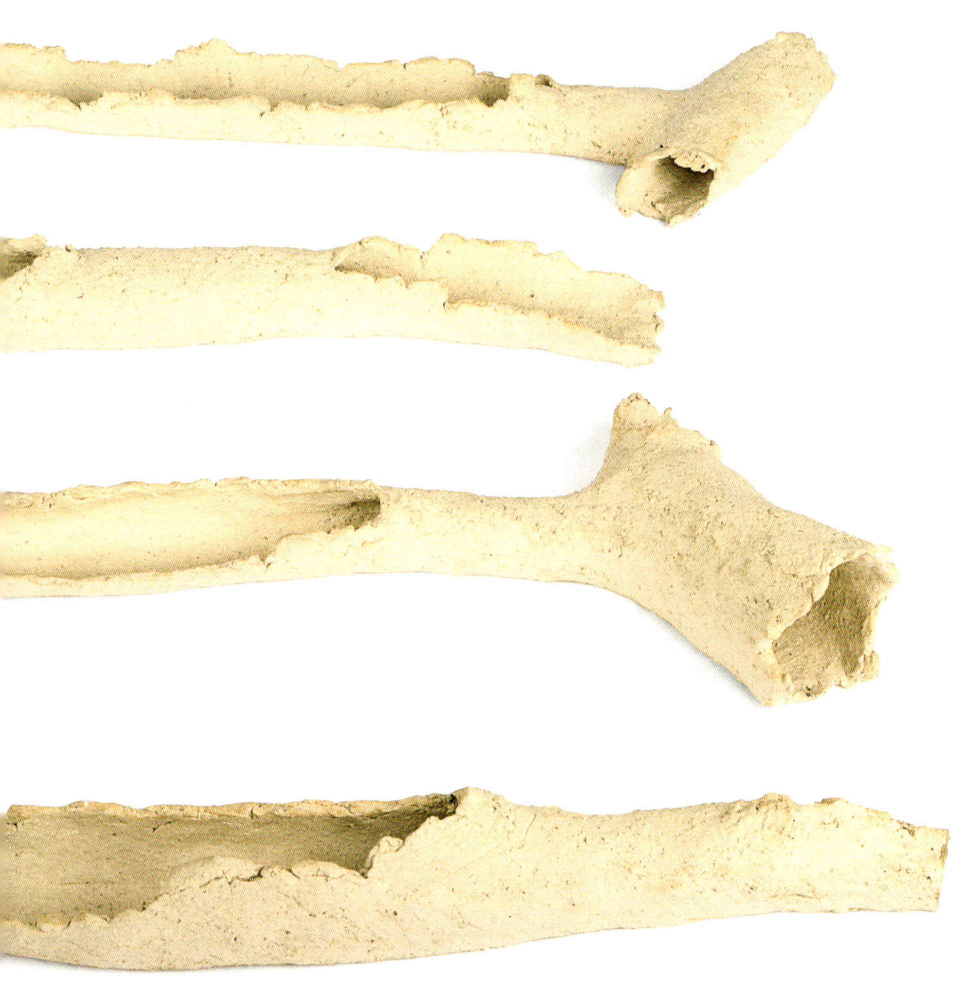

2 Physeter
1989
2 Stück, gebrannter und glasierter Ton
12 x 65 x 11 cm

2 potwhales
1989
2 pieces, fired and glazed clay
12 x 65 x 11 cm

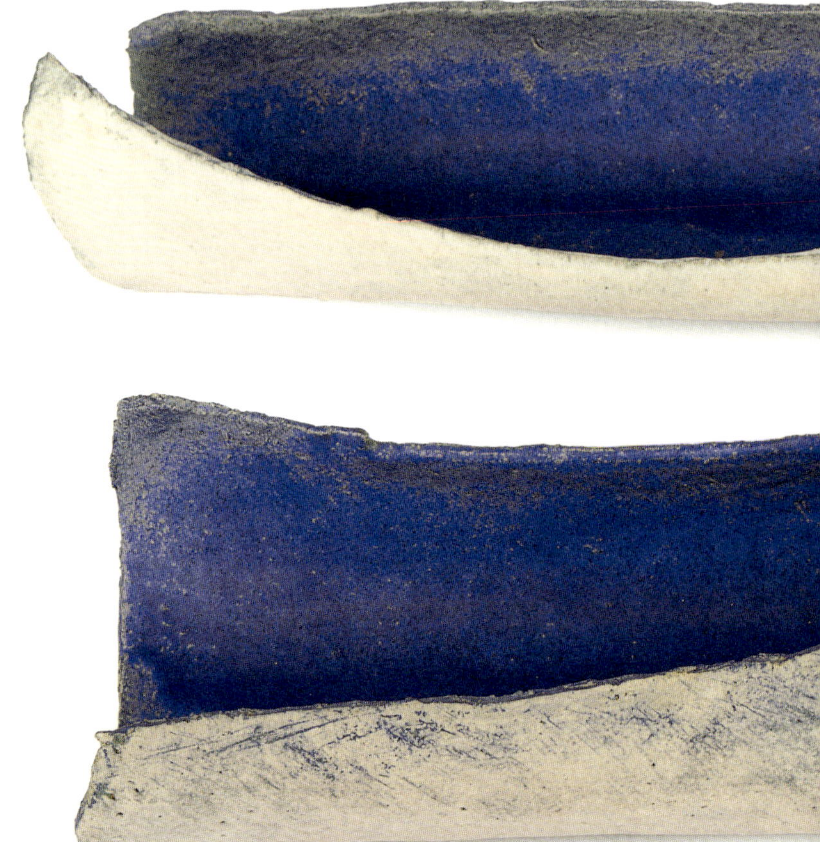

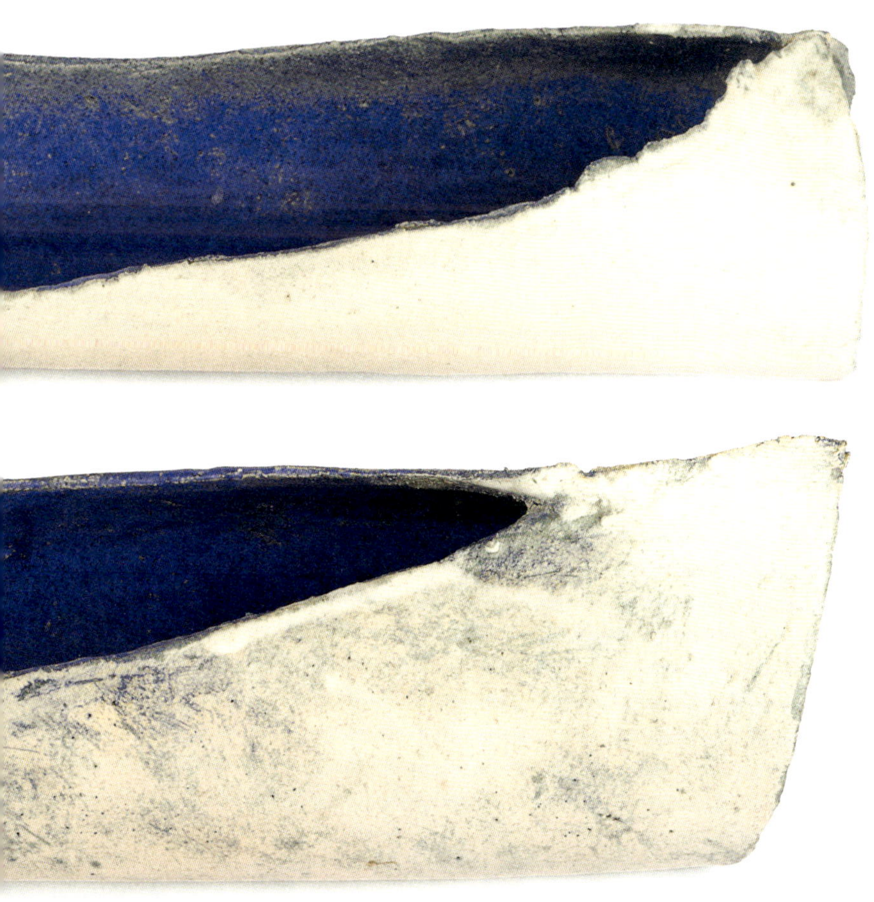

mittwochs
2010
Bleistift auf Papier
70 x 50 cm

Wednesdays
2010
pencil on paper
70 x 50 cm

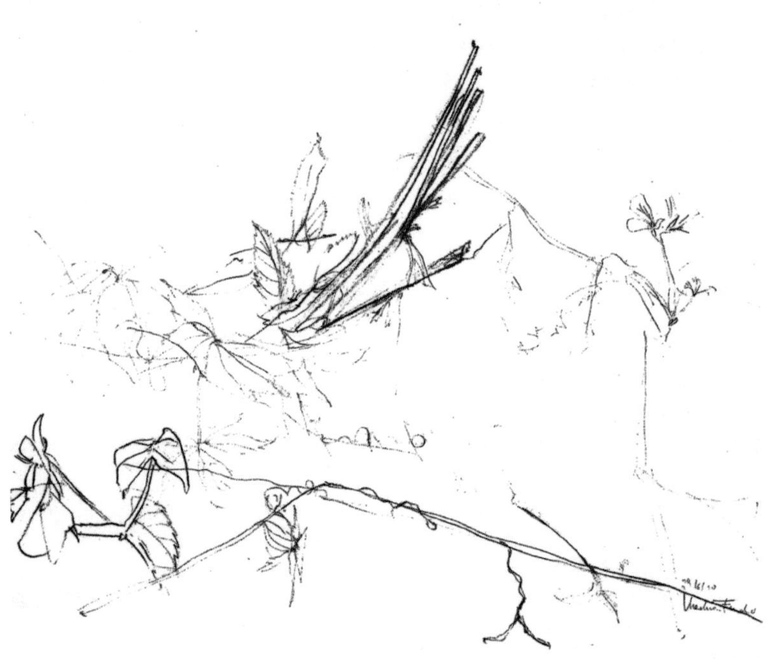

montags
2010
Bleistift auf Papier
70 x 50 cm

Mondays
2010
pencil on paper
70 x 50 cm

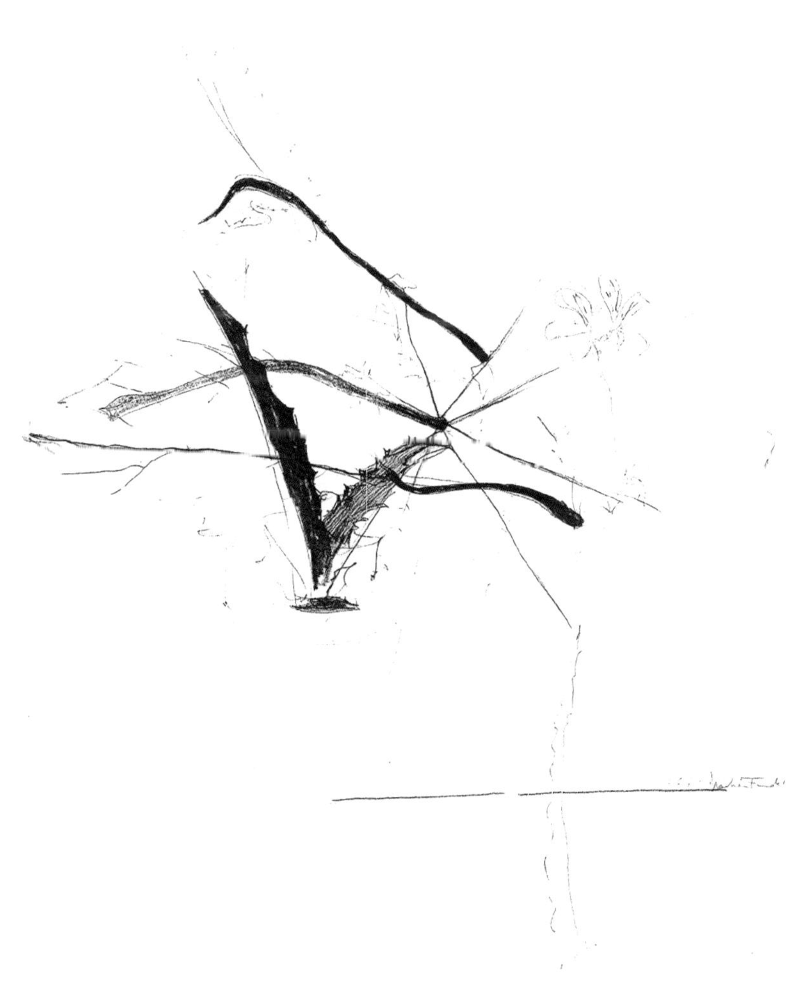

Astplatte
1992
gebrannter und glasierter Ton
12 x 20 x 12 cm

branch platter
1992
fired and glazed clay
12 x 20 x 12 cm

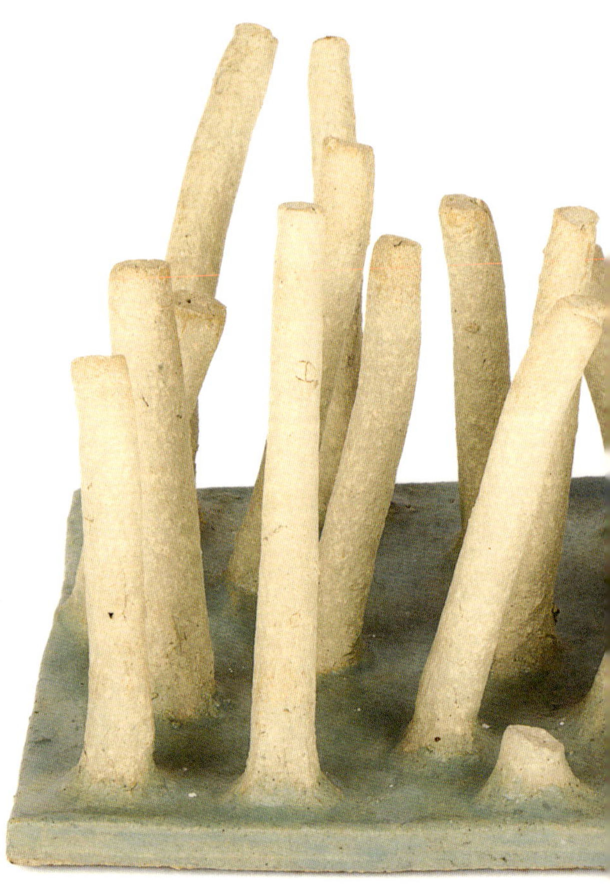

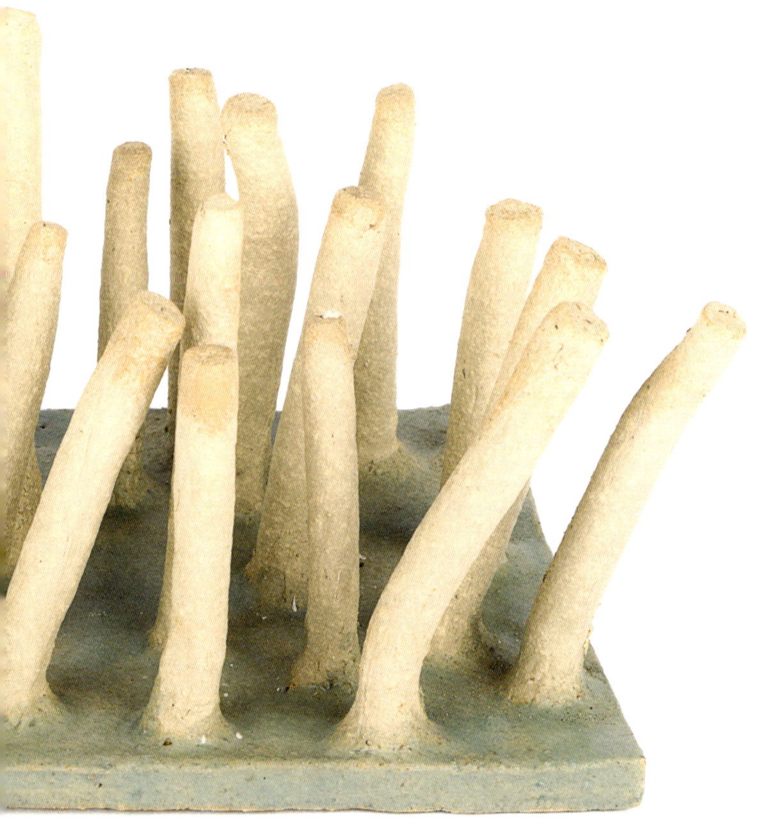

Burg Bonbon
aus der Serie *Bonbon*
1995
gebrannter und engobierter Ton
20 x 50 x 50 cm

castle bonbon
from the *bonbon* series
1995
fired and engobed clay
20 x 50 x 50 cm

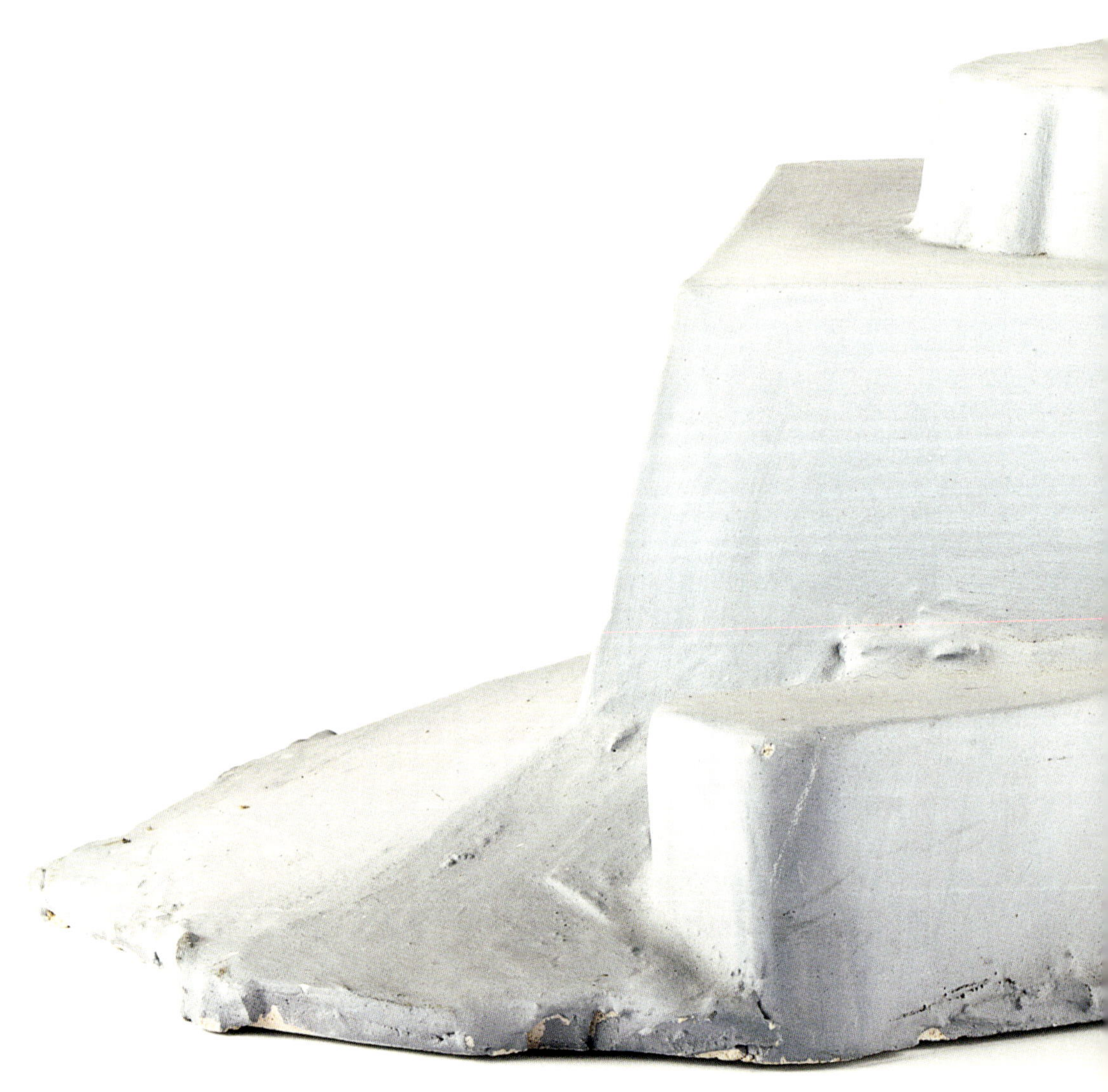

Seegras
1996
gebrannter und engobierter Ton
20 x 40 x 40 cm

sea grass
1996
fired and engobed clay
20 x 40 x 40 cm

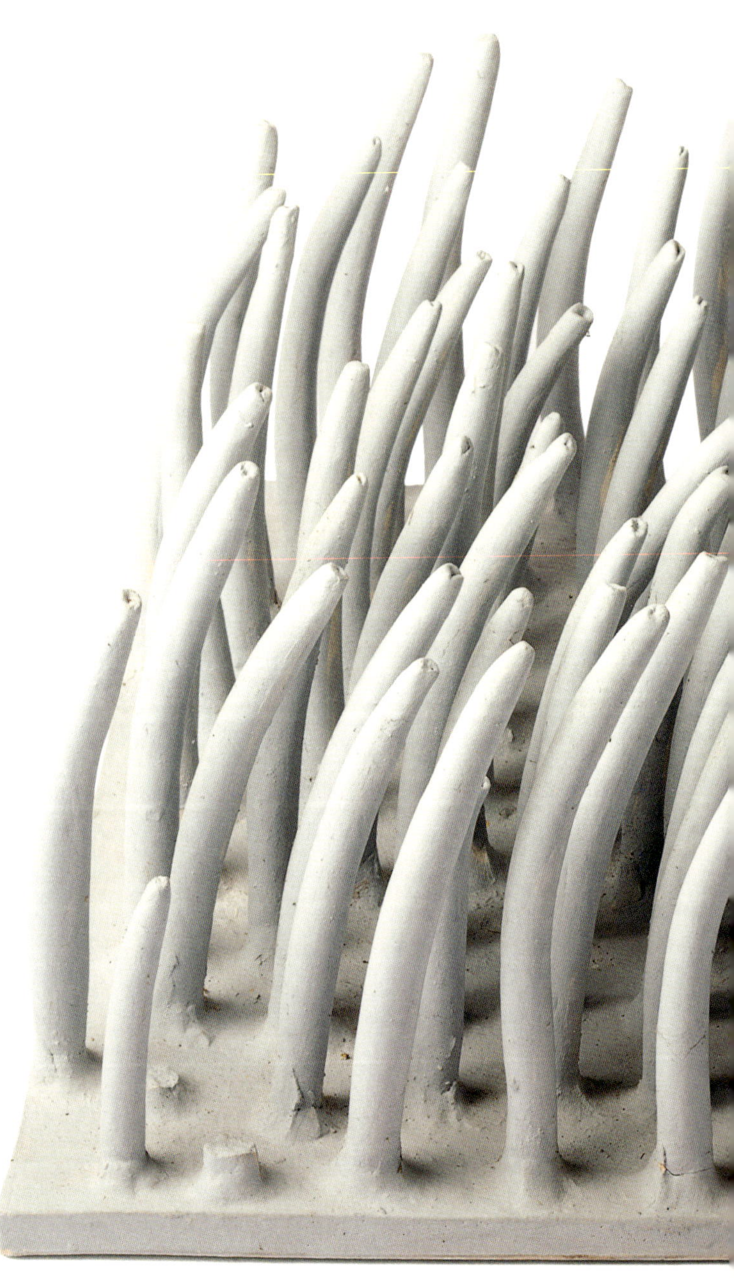

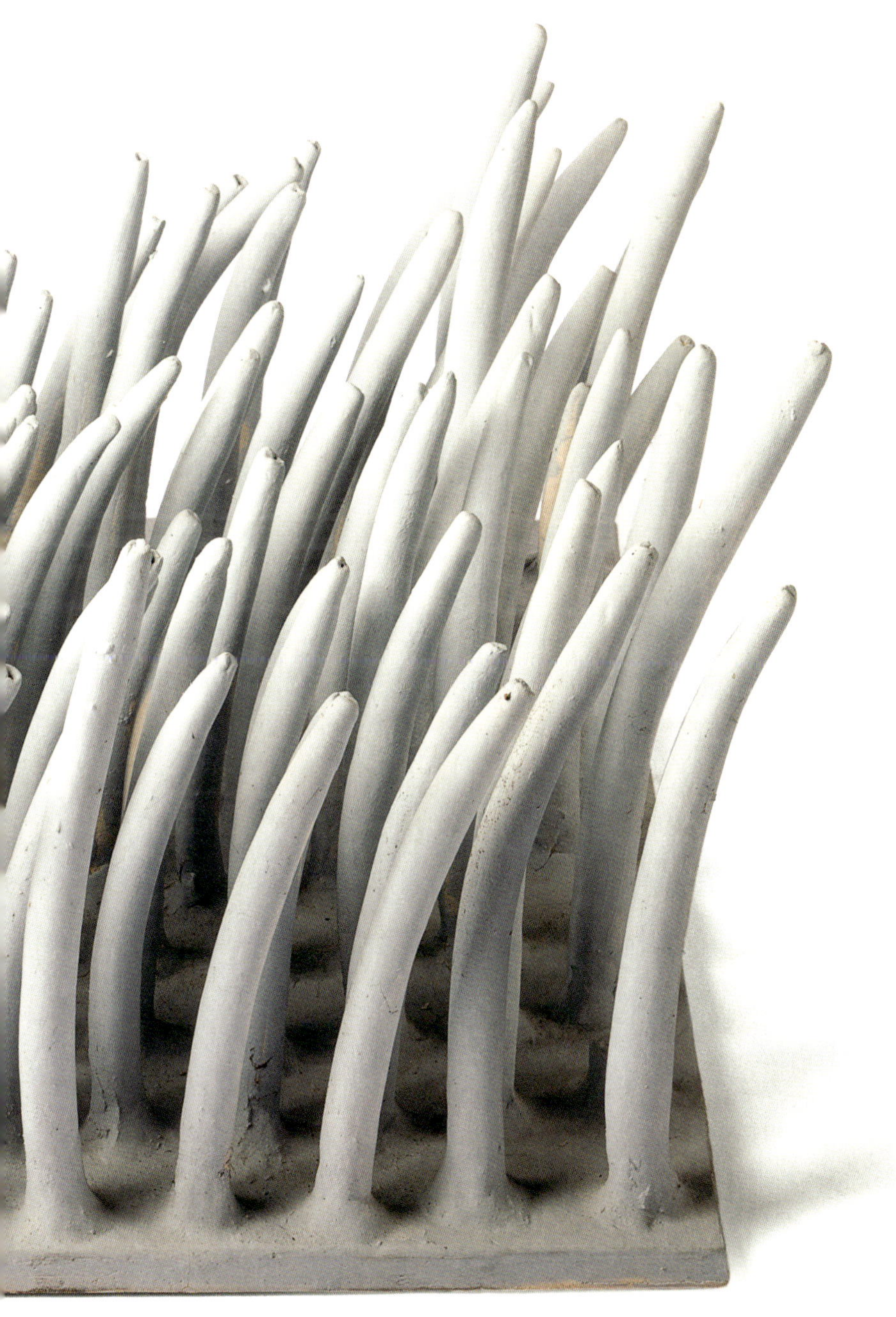

3 Badener Wadln
1996
gebrannter Ton mit Lüsterglasur
höchstes Stück 50 cm

3 Baden calves
1996
fired clay with luster glaze
highest piece 50 cm

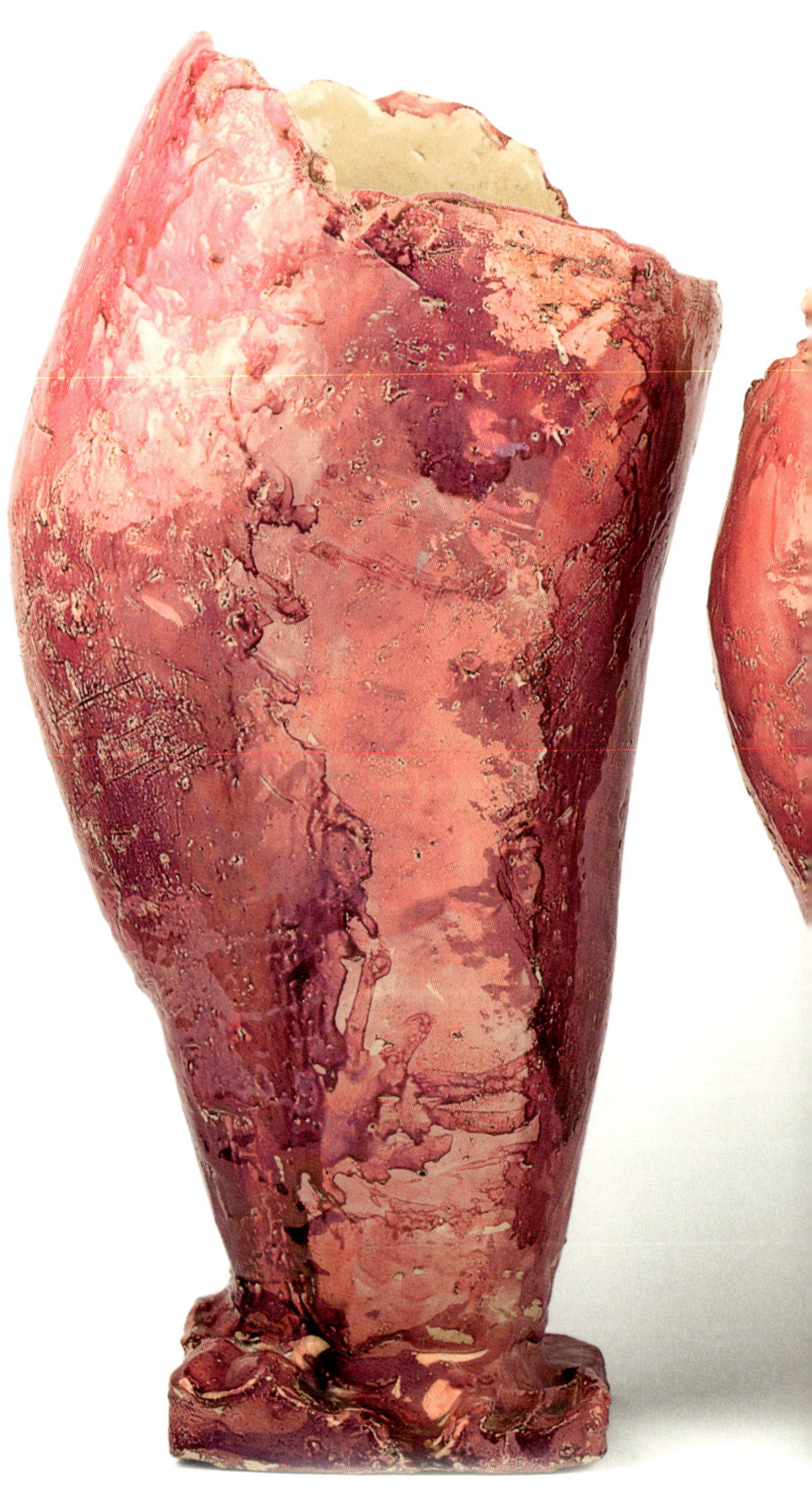

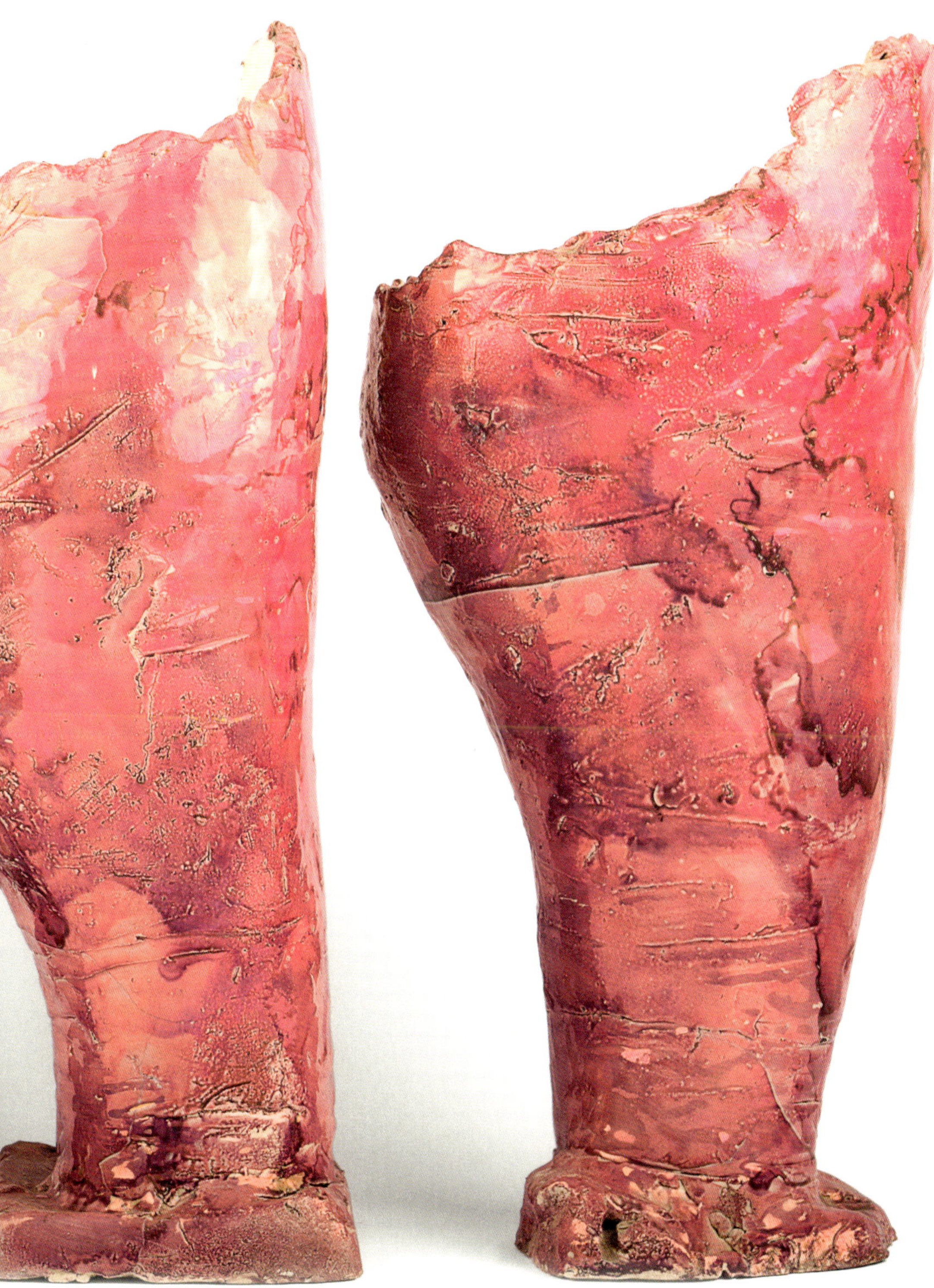

Tulpenziegel
2001
3-teilig, gebrannter und glasierter Ton
5 x 90 x 40 cm

tulip tiles
2001
3-piece, fired and glazed clay
5 x 90 x 40 cm

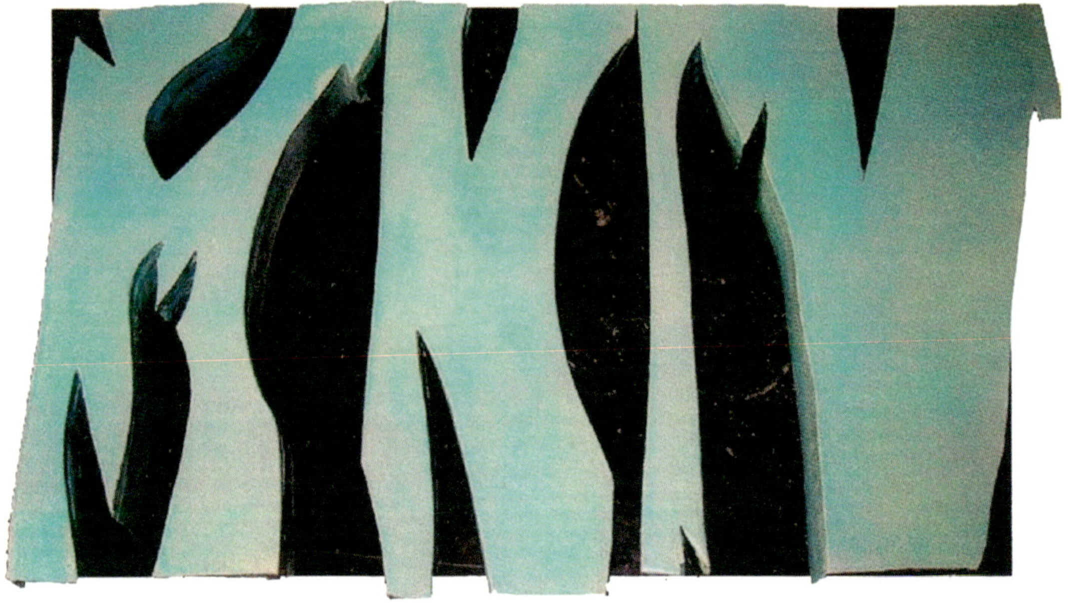

Renée Gadsden

The Garden of Earthly Delights

Altissima quaeque flumina minimo sono labiuntur [still waters run deep]
Quintus Curtius Rufus, History of Alexander the Great
(Book VII, chapter 4, paragraph 13)

Martina Funder is looking for freedom. She approaches each new person, situation and event with an attitude of attentive watchfulness. Inspiration for her art, Funder is proud to explain, comes only from her every day encounters. Her work is not pretentious, nor does it proselytize. Funder supplies us with seemingly simple renderings of things as they are, filtered through her artistic and emotional eye. She has invented a language based on intuitive rules, logically and systematically applied, although not necessarily discernible to the viewer's gaze.

Her first formal training in art was at the Academy of Fine Arts Vienna under Gustav Hessing in the master class for painting. The emphasis was on looking directly and intensely at nature, and following what was revealed there. This strictness of approach has remained a major influence in Funder's way of handling her preferred medium of expression, ceramics. She says that this background in drawing causes her to use clay in an architectonical way, applying concepts of above and below, thinking in grids, lines and structures. This can be seen clearly in works such as *Die Mauern (the walls*, 2008), where she molded and bent the clay as if she wanted to draw with it, or in *panorama* (2010), long rows of thin ceramic jagged peaks, which give form to an experience of looking out at foggy mountains in the distance at a high altitude.

Her interest in the aspects of art that could be discovered through academic discipline led her further to the University of Art and Design Linz, to study ceramics with Günther Praschak. After these study times living in Vienna and Linz, she set up her home and studio in Baden near Vienna, where a spacious garden and atelier rooms provide ample ground for her ceramic ovens, music instruments, easels and painting materials, and all the other tools of her trade. Funder herself is a drawing instructor, and holds classes and workshops in ceramics. She tries to be as sensitive to her students as she is to her inner voice, remarking that although her education provided her with the skills to use materials to achieve artistic goals, the emancipation process from what she learned at university has been a lifelong struggle. With a smile, she wonders aloud if perhaps it would have been better not to have indulged in formal training at all.

This kind of subtle irony can be seen in sculptures such as *Der verkaufte Berg (the sold mountain*, 2013) which was inspired by the desperation of Austrian villages in a time of economic crisis for income and the relentless greed of companies hungry for marketing opportunities. Some few years ago, in southern Austria, mountain peaks were "sold off." The historical name of the mountain was replaced with a company name in exchange for badly needed cash injections into the municipal treasuries. The title also consciously evokes the title of Bedřich Smetana's brilliant 19th century social commentary, the opera *Die verkaufte Braut (The Bartered Bride)*.

Funder has a critical view of the machinations of today's global markets, and comments on them in her very personal way in works such as Taro; taro is a "worthless" plant that grows on the sides of the road in southern India and serves as food for the poorer segments of the population. *Badener Wadln (Baden calves*, 1996) was inspired by the many thick and sturdy legs of the overfed visitors that parade on the *Strandbad* (Baden City Beach) in summer. In this piece, without being overtly political, Funder still manages to comment on the situation in Baden itself, a place struggling to find a new identity beyond the narrow boundaries of its history as a Biedermeier watering hole turned 21st century spa town for those suffering from often self-induced lifestyle diseases. In the work *Über den Tellerrand schauen (look beyond the end of one's nose*, 1996) Funder once again emphasizes the need for us, in the West, to gain meaningful perspectives on the world at large.

In her ceramics, one can witness a range of clay and techniques that testify to Funder's joy in experimenting, although she claims not to be a "material fetishist." Porcelain she avoids as being too fragile, but has experimented with engobe in her 1995 *bonbon* series. Funder plays consciously with the coloration of her objects through skillful manipulation of the temperature in the ceramic ovens during firing. She knows her area of interest in depth, not only as an artist but also as a craftsperson. She is a designer and builder of tile stoves. Such masonry heaters are small masterworks of ceramic ingenuity and know-how, each one unique. Funder learned this skill at the Fessler Oven and Fireplace Manufactory, a potter's workshop founded in the Baroque era that was a purveyor to the imperial and royal Austrian court. It is still run by the founding family today – the family of her mother's forbearers. She lived in the center of Vienna at the Fessler workshop on Mozartplatz while studying at the fine arts academy.

Although her works once described by her ceramics professor as "brittle, stand-offish," this is a misleading observation. Martina Funder does have very passionate sides. True to her nature, however, she feels no need to display these sides of herself in obvious ways. She is a relentless wanderer, a seeker after truth in herself and in the world around her. When not at work in her studio, or with her family, friends or students, you can probably find Funder on the way to the top of a mountain. She looks for the deeper, higher, more profound view, in herself and in nature. She wanders the mountain landscapes of her native Austria, and prefers to make many day and week foot marches into the heart of the wilderness. She has explored the delta of the Danube for weeks at a time on several different occasions. The terrains of Nepal, India, Tibet, Egypt, Morocco, and her newest exploratory destination, Peru, are all absorbed into her consciousness in a very direct way: slowly, through the sensation and effect of the landscape on her body. Insights into the soul of hiking gained as a result of walking.

Martina Funder becomes impassioned when she describes herself as being captivated by forms. Certain forms take possession of her and don't let go until she has processed them in her art. She emphasizes the haptic aspect of her approach: "Ich könnte nie mit einem Material arbeiten, das ich nicht angreifen kann" (I could never work with a material that I couldn't touch). Her work is always about what she has experienced ("Was ich darstelle, hat dann immer mit Erlebtem zu tun"). For example, *Sturmäste (storm branches*, 1991) and *Astplatte (branch platter*, 1992) depict cut off tree branches and limbs that represent how Funder felt after a knee operation. Gargoyles and nightmares are evoked by her *Grausige Schädel (horrible heads*, 2013), heavy ceramic skulls in dark colors with eerie and slightly threatening knobs and protuberances. This work was evoked by the frightening and sad process of witnessing her mother succumb to Alzheimer's disease.

We also often see in her oeuvre the sensations and experiences of her immense and prolonged wanderings. Funder defines *Seegras (sea grass*, 1996) as giving her a feeling of ease in the water as the wind moves across it. She also likes to play with the scale of the objects she observes. The *Ahornsamen (maple tree seeds*, 2003) or the *Tulpenziegel (tulip tiles*, 2001) are many times larger than their original counterparts. Funder explains that this magnification is her way to pay homage to the beauty of nature ("Ich setze dem Löwenzahnblatt wegen seiner tollen Form ein Denkmal, indem ich es vergrößert habe"). The 2006 *Gewickelt (colied)* series (such as *Nicht links gewickelt; Nicht links gedreht; Cut, Gedreht, Gewickelt / not coiled to the left; not turned to the left; cut, turned, coiled)*, small white ceramic forms, coiled and rolled and set tightly together on a platter, are a direct interpretation of the stylized lion's manes she saw on temple statues in Nepal.

In her extensive photographic oeuvre, Funder combines her passion for experiencing nature firsthand with her artist's eye as well. When she travels, a camera is her companion as well as a sketchpad. The photographic documentation of her global ramblings is lovingly organized in bound books that line the shelves of her study. Common issues and the ordinary in extraordinary places characterize Funder's photography, a William Eggleston approach to the trivial and banal. A close examination shows how thoroughly chosen are the compositions of seemingly random situations and scenes. She adjusts himself to whatever comes across her camera, and in doing so cuts out a small piece of reality, transforming it into a work of art because of its individual and unique perspective. The most delightful aspect of these photo books are that they are private memory grazing grounds, little cabinets of curiosities intended only for Funder's own perusal, not for exhibition or public display. She also writes travel diaries, which she also only uses for her own reflection.

Perhaps Martina Funder is somewhere deep inside inspired by her great-grandfather Ludwig Funder, a confectioner from Graz who made a journeyman's walking tour throughout Europe from 1862 to 1869. He wrote down his experiences, which were published under the title *Aus meinem Burschenleben (From My Lad's Life)*. The historian Michael Mitterauer has called the account "völlig banalen Alltag eines Zuckerbäckers" (a fully

Weg zum Pass Nara-La, Grenze Nepal–Tibet
track to pass Nara-La, border Nepal–Tibet

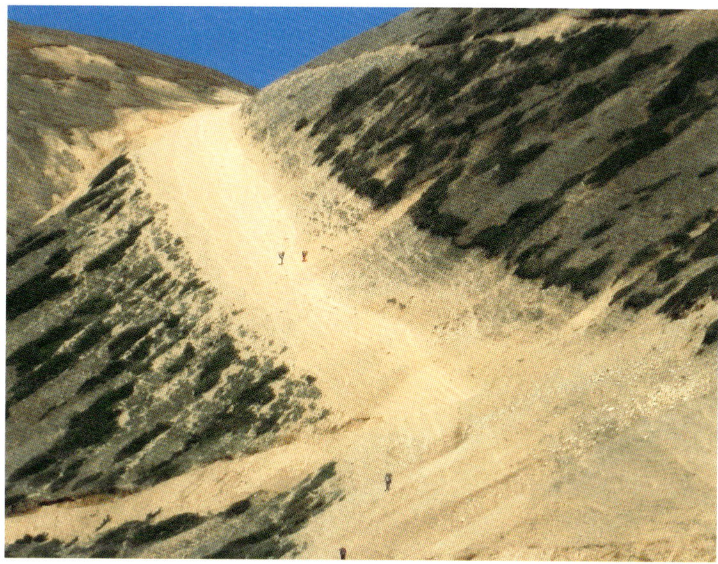

banal everyday life of a confectioner), but for other sensibilities, it is an exhilarating peak into one man's confrontation with adventure, curiosity, and ardor. At the very latest since the Jeff Koons created the 1988 sculpture series *Banality*, it is clear that embracing the quotidian is an aspect of contemporary art that cannot be thought away anymore. Funder is not afraid to do so, and fearlessly and consistently produces works that embody the philosophy of E. F. Schumacher, inspired by his mentor Leopold Kohr, that "small is beautiful." She describes herself as an optimist who has few material goods, but is deeply satisfied with her life. Her grandfather, the Catholic publicist Friedrich Funder, strived in his efforts to encourage people to search for inner peace and harmony with one another. His books line her shelves, in between other writers whose thoughts have helped shape her approach to art, such as Fernand Braudel's *Civilisation matérielle, économie et capitalisme – xve–xviiie siècle: Les structures du quotidien (Der Alltag)*, or Christine Busta's *Einsilbig ist die Sprache der Nacht*, or Cecilia Lindqvist's seminal study of the Chinese culture of writing, *Hanzi Wangguo or the Kingdom of Characters (Eine Welt aus Zeichen)*. When asked what her perspective is on Catholicism, Funder answered, totally refreshingly: "Alles ist so schön, alles was ich sehen kann. Ich möchte das festhalten, um es allen zu zeigen" (Everything is so beautiful, everything that I can see. I want to capture that to show everyone).

Considering that Martina Funder has so much family history to carry makes her almost naïve and direct ceramic works even more enjoyable. She has a deeply rooted sense of self that carries over into her art with quiet dignity. She lets us discover small moments of wonder, as if with the eyes of a child: "Etwas Schönes entdecken und es dann auch mitteilen zu können, dieses Wollen treibt mich zu mener Arbeit an." Martina Funder is a quiescent artistic oracle, enhancing our perception of the marvels of this garden we all share, the garden of earthly delights.

schräges Stück
2003
gebrannter und glasierter Ton
25 x 70 x 20 cm

quirky piece
2003
fired and glazed clay
25 x 70 x 20 cm

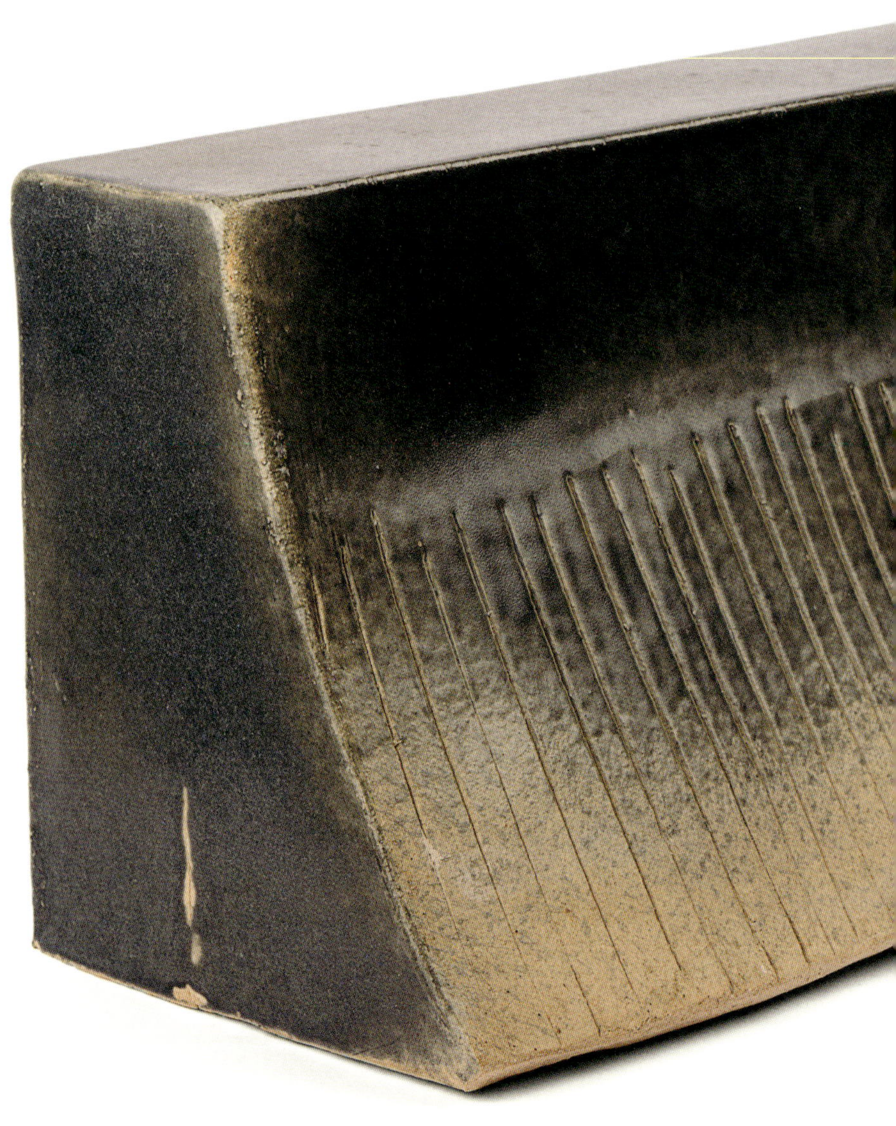

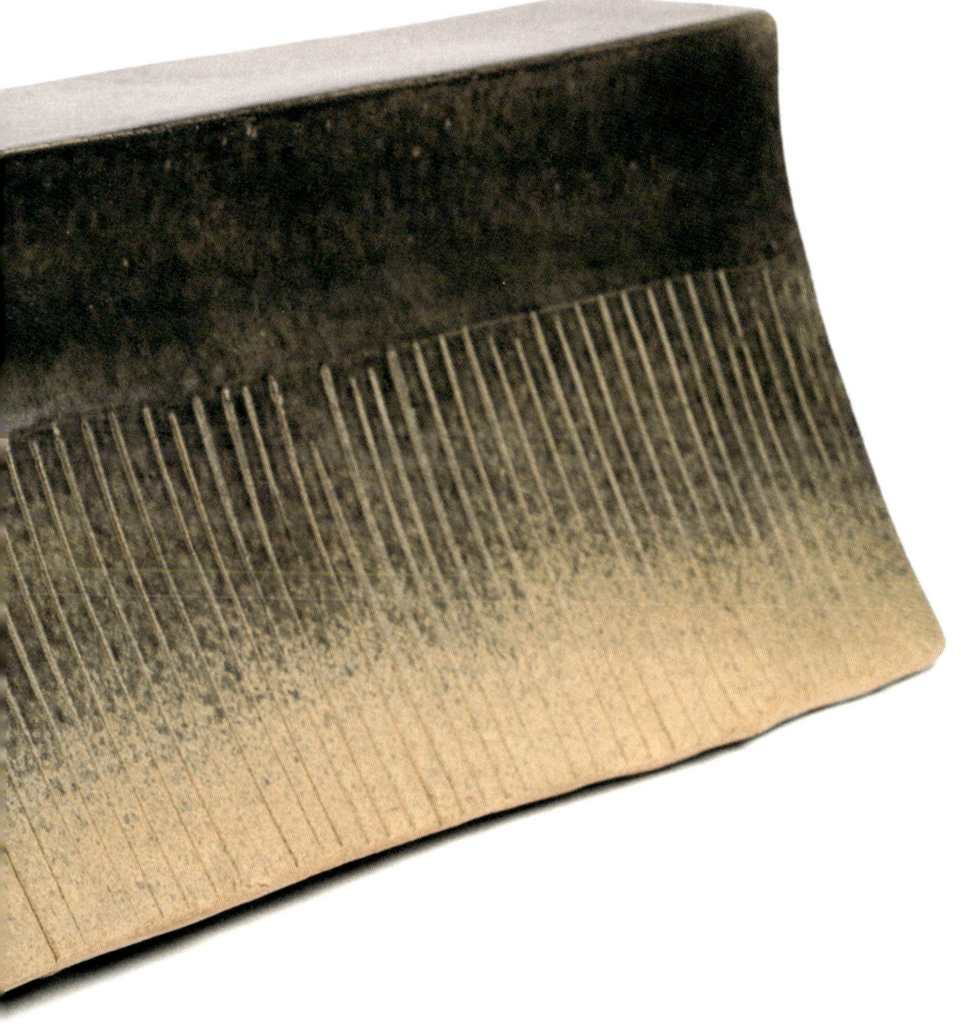

verpackter Ton
2002
gebrannter und glasierter Ton
10 x 28 x 12,5 cm

packaged clay
2002
fired and glazed clay
10 x 28 x 12.5 cm

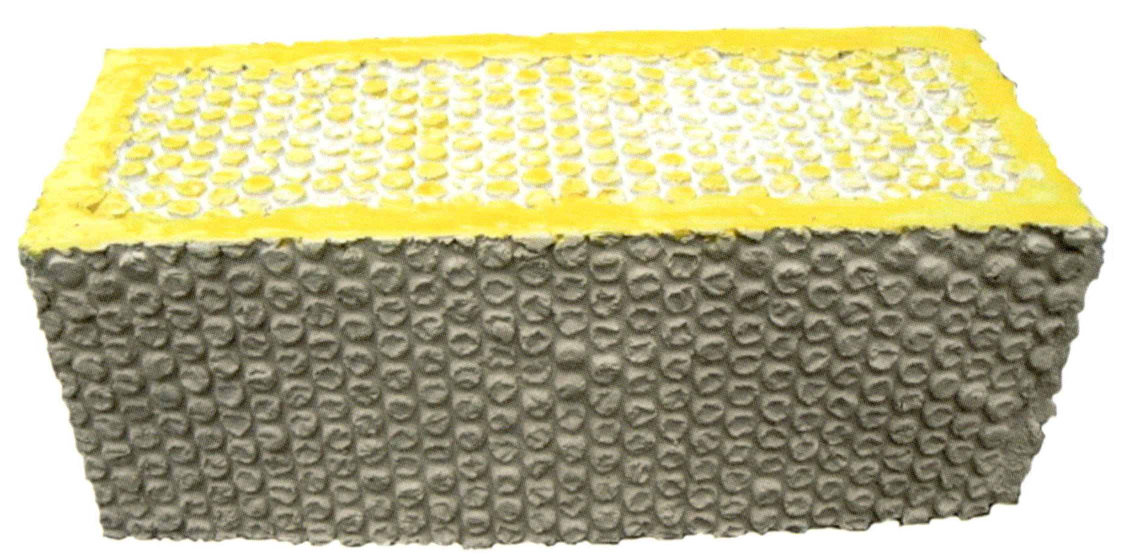

orange Kiwis
2002
gebrannter und glasierter Ton
1 x 40 x 40 cm

orange kiwis
2002
fired and glazed clay
1 x 40 x 40 cm

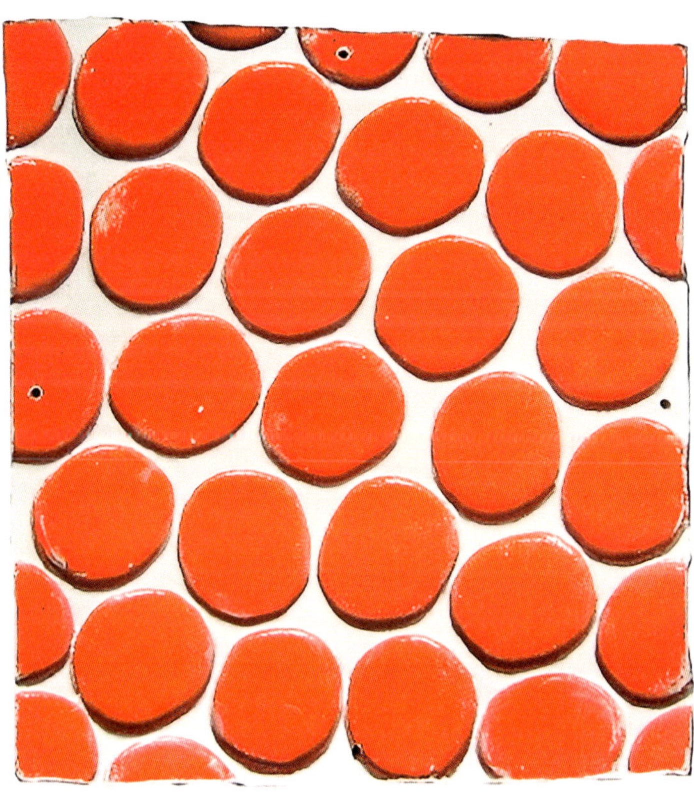

globalisierte Kiwis
2002
6-teilig, gebrannter und glasierter Ton
à 1 x 40 x 40 cm

globalized kiwis
2002
6-piece, fired and glazed clay
1 x 40 x 40 cm each

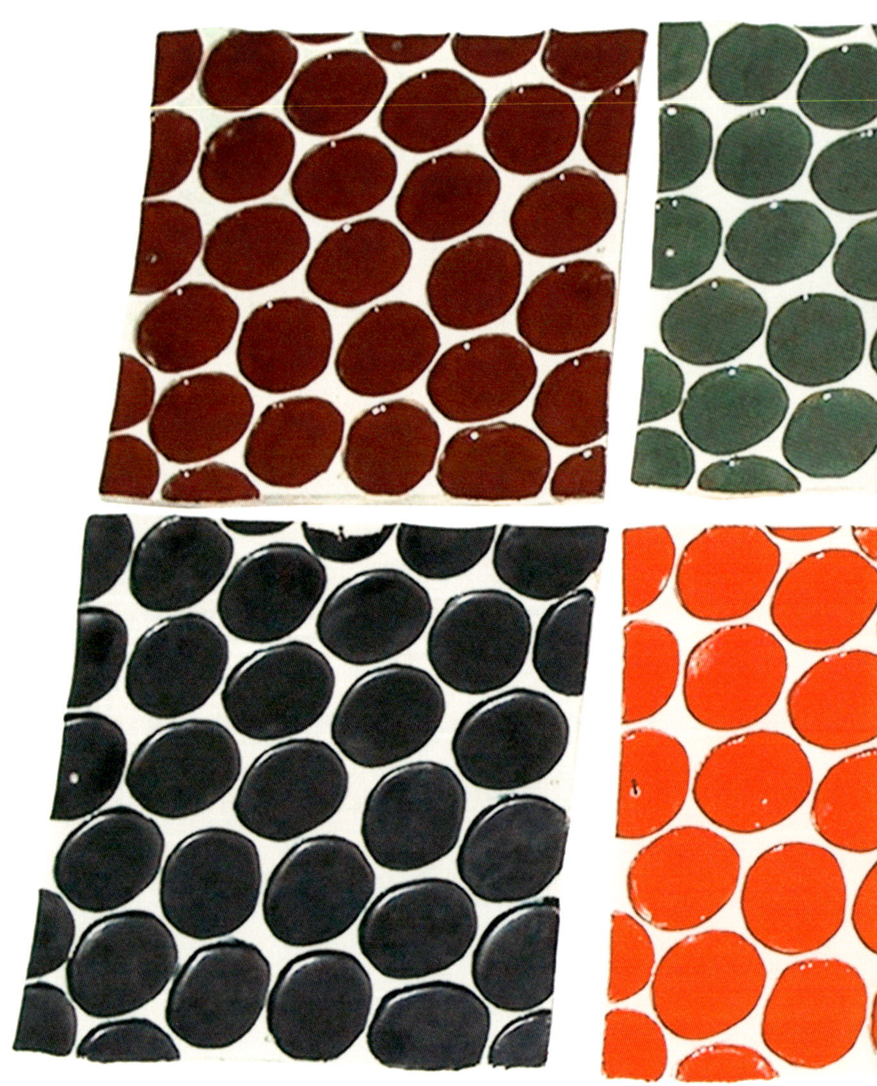

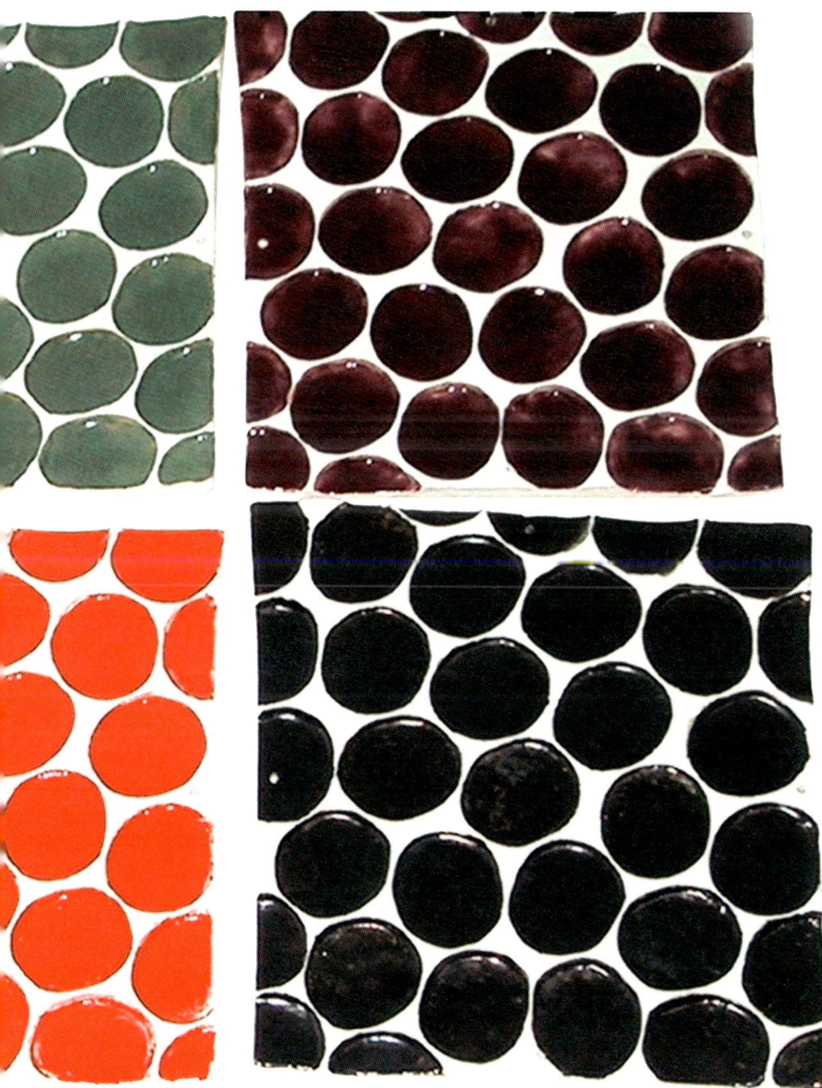

Löwenzahnblatt
2002
gebrannter und glasierter Ton
60 x 35 x 30 cm

dandelion leaf
2002
fired and glazed clay
60 x 35 x 30 cm

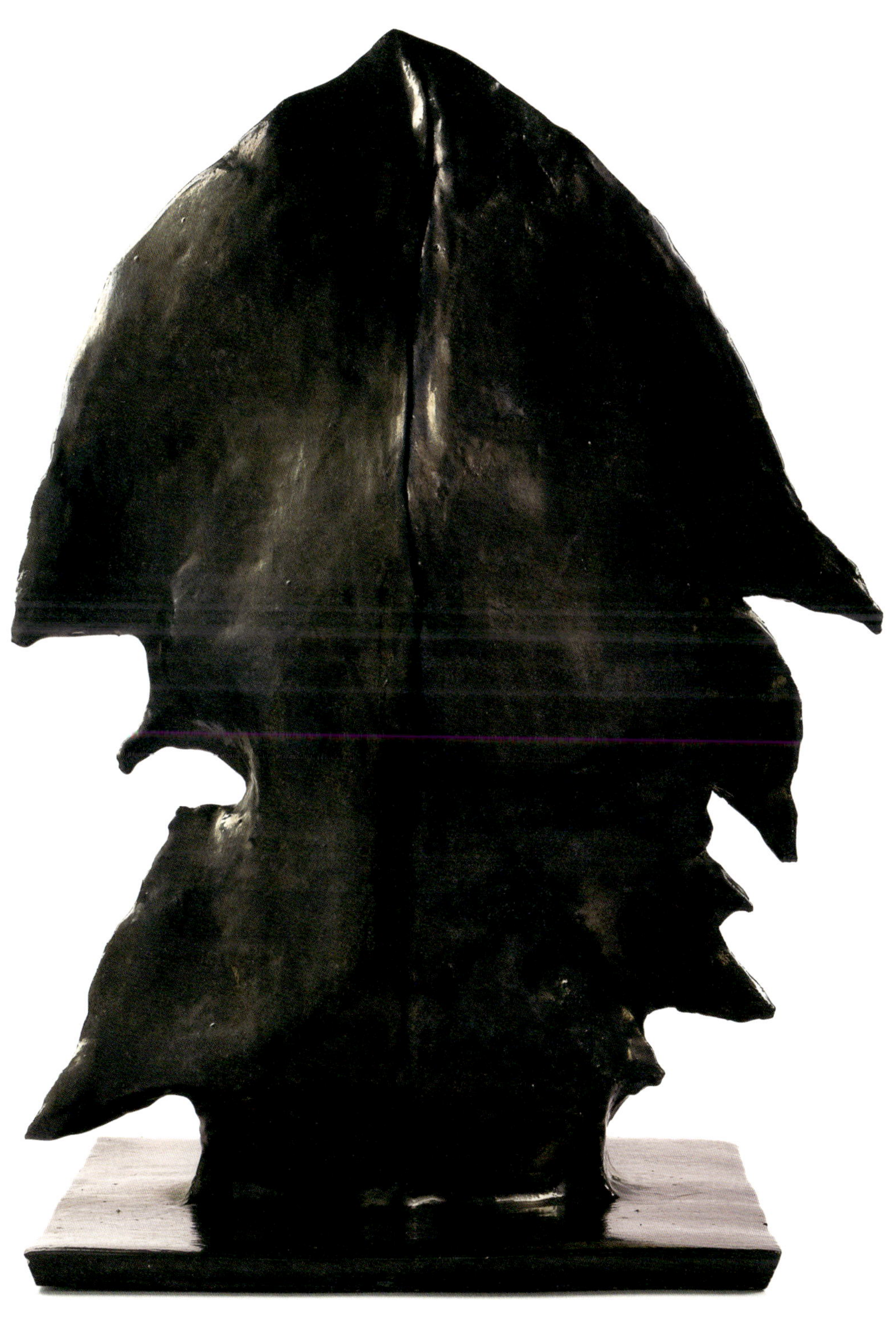

Knospenkugel
2004
gebrannter und glasierter Ton
15 x 28 x 28 cm

orb of buds
2004
fired and glazed clay
15 x 28 x 28 cm

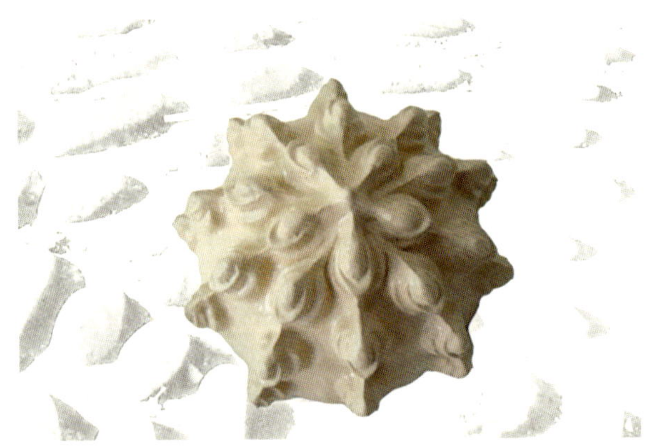

Stripes
2006
gebrannter und engobierter Ton
2 x 40 x 30 cm

stripes
2006
fired and engobed clay
2 x 40 x 30 cm

Locken eines nepalesischen Löwen
2006
2 Stück, gebrannter und engobierter Ton
à 3 x 30 x 40 cm

curls of a Nepalese lion
2006
2 pieces, fired and engobed clay
3 x 30 x 40 cm each

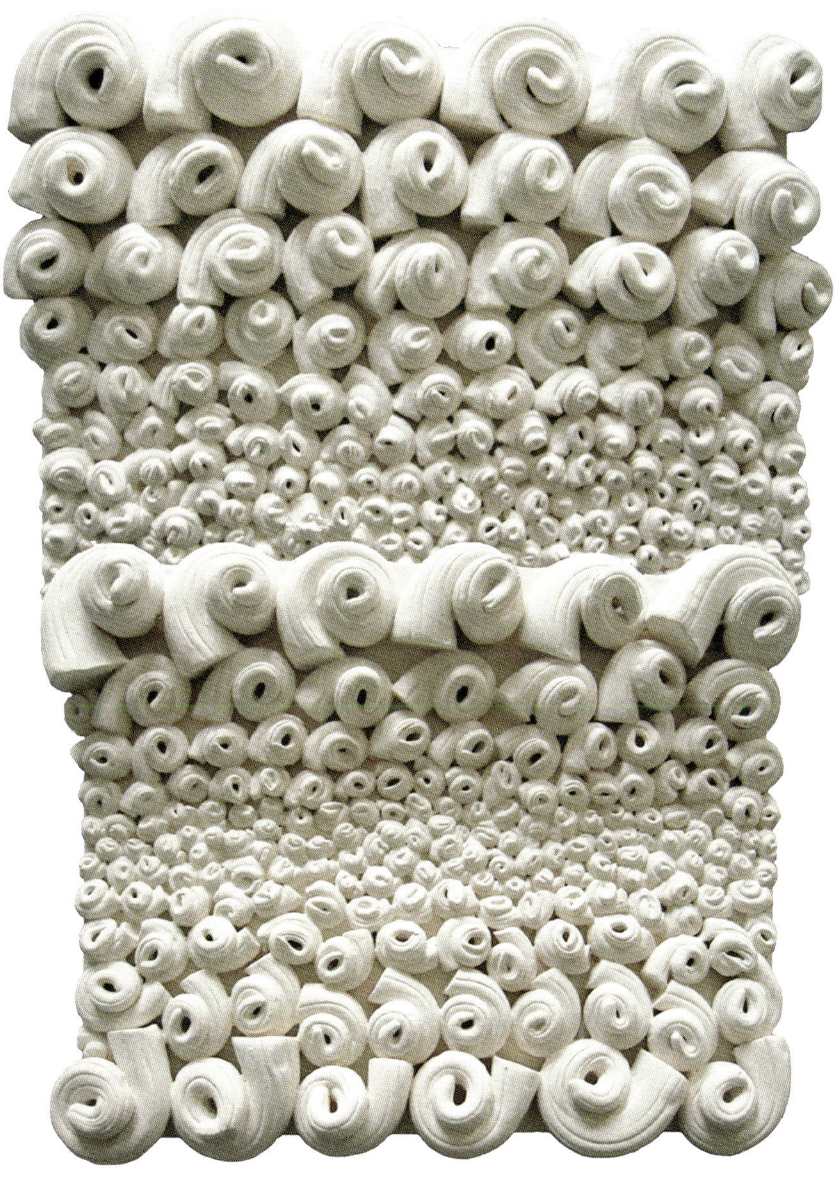

Locken eines nepalesischen Löwen, Kathmandu
curls of a Nepalese lion, Kathmandu

Kolam, Südindien
Kolam, Southern India

Vischnu/Schildkröte, Kathmandu
Vishnu/turtle, Kathmandu

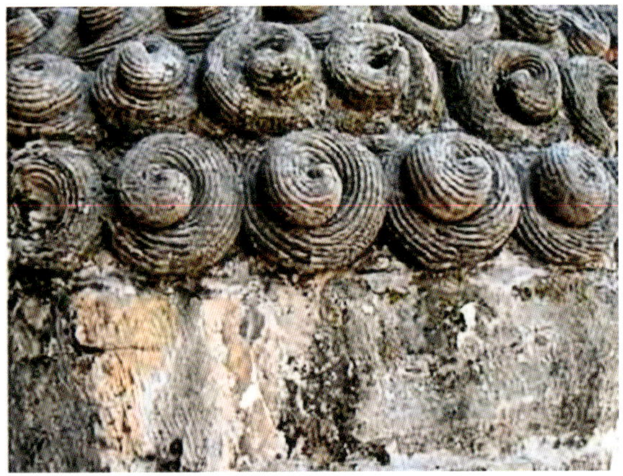

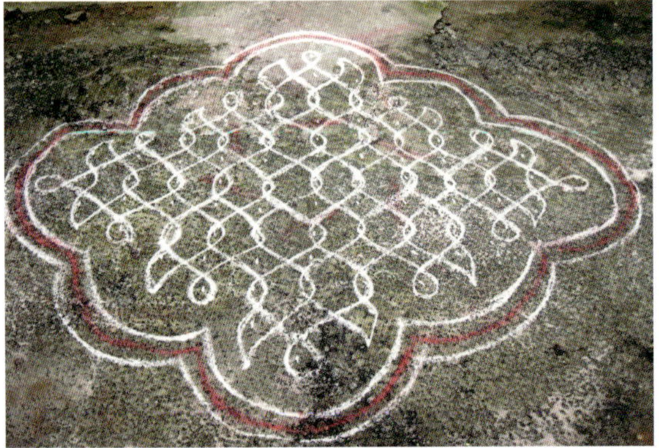

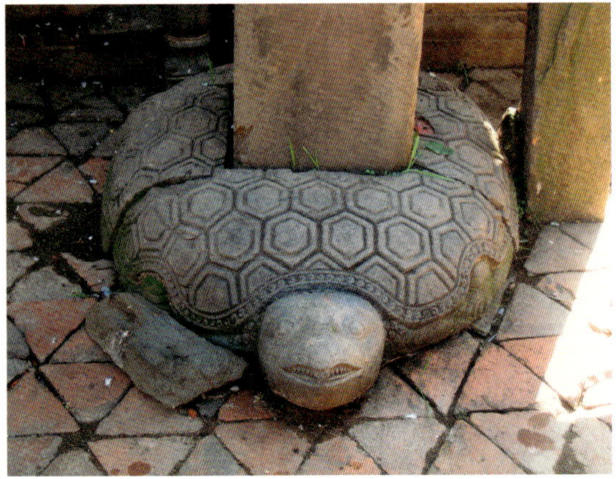

Hartwig Knack

Rhythmus – Statik – Konstruktion

Drei wesentliche Aspekte der keramischen Arbeit von Martina Funder

Das facettenreiche Formenrepertoire von Martina Funders Keramiken reicht vom Linear-Geometrischen bis zum Organisch-Vegetabilen. Die Oberflächenbeschaffenheit ihrer Objekte ist rau oder grob, glatt oder glasiert. Die Natur mit ihrer Fülle an Mustern, Rhythmen und Farben liefert der Künstlerin immer wieder aufs Neue Impulse für ihre Kunst. Dabei integriert Funder in ihre Werke immer tagesaktuelle Themen aus Politik und Gesellschaft, die sie betreffen oder betroffen machen.

So erinnern manche Werke der Künstlerin einerseits an modulare Stahlkonstruktionen, wie sie in der Hochhausarchitektur Verwendung finden, andererseits scheinen sie abstrahierte Abbilder organischer Formen zu sein. Funder spielt mit dem vermeintlichen Gegensatzpaar des Organischen und Geometrischen, stellt Zusammenhänge und Analogien her und versucht, ordnend einzugreifen. Heraus kommen Werke wie etwa *Units aus Korea*, eine Arbeit, die als ein kritischer Verweis auf den bereits über zwei Jahrzehnte andauernden Bauboom in weiten Teilen Asiens gelesen werden kann. Bauern wurden systematisch von ihrem Land vertrieben und unzählige Wanderarbeiter versklavt. Die Arbeit *Modul 1-2-3* zeigt einen Blick in die Regelmäßigkeit und Symmetrie eines mathematisch durchkonstruierten Körpers und weckt Assoziationen zu einem monumentalen Stahlbeton-Skelettbau. Ein Blick, der durchaus auch dem Inneren einer biologischen Zellstruktur entlehnt sein könnte.

Martina Funders Objekte erschließen sich grundsätzlich erst auf den zweiten Blick. Ihre Motive findet sie im Alltag. Aus zunächst interessant erscheinenden Themen und Fundstücken entwickelt sie ihre Ideen. Knospenkugeln, vom Sturm abgebrochene Äste, ein Holzscheit und ein Löwenzahnblatt erlangen durch Transformationsprozesse und Dimensionsverschiebungen zu plastischen Keramiken neue haptische Qualitäten und gewinnen veränderte inhaltliche Ebenen. So war zum Beispiel ein Presseartikel Anlass für die Künstlerin, sich kritisch zu Auswüchsen des Kapitalismus zu äußern: Als die Wiener Tageszeitung *Der Standard* 2001 über neuseeländische Obstbauern berichtete, die im Begriff waren, eine neue Kiwi-Sorte mit rotem Fruchtfleisch für den weltweiten Markt zu züchten, entwickelte Funder spontan ihre Arbeiten *gelber Kiwiziegel* und *globalisierte Kiwis* in den Farben Gelb, Bronze, Rot, Dunkelrot, Dunkelgrün sowie Schwarzmatt und -glänzend. Die Künstlerin ironisiert damit die Strategien der Werbebranche, indem sie ihrerseits eine erweiterte Farbpalette als aufreizende Neuigkeit präsentiert. So persifliert Funder einen der vorrangingen Wesenszüge des Kapitalismus, die maximale Gewinnorientierung durch Entwicklung vermeintlich neuer Waren.

Als Lebenszeichen, als Spiegel von Schnelligkeit, aber auch als Metapher von Ruhe und Rationalität ist die Linie in allen Kulturkreisen bekannt. Ganz frühe künstlerische Äußerungen des Menschen sind schon linear ausgeführt: Denken wir nur an die Felszeichnungen der Urmenschen. Jeder von uns hat als Kind in Strichzeichnungen seine ersten Erlebnisse auf Papier gekritzelt. Die Linie, die Grundlage jedes menschlichen Gestaltens ist, begleitet auch viele Werke Martina Funders. Manchmal orientiert sich die Künstlerin am Vorbild der Natur wie etwa in der Arbeit *Panorama*, wo sie sich von der Stimmung nebelverhangener Hügelketten vor der Kulisse eines Sonnenaufgangs hat inspirieren lassen.

In anderen Werken bezieht sich ihre Linie auf symmetrische Muster und Strukturen wie bei einem tamilischen Kolam, einer Zeichnung, die Frauen im Süden Indiens auf dem Boden vor ihrem Hauseingang zum Schutz vor bösen Geistern regelmäßig erneuern. In der Arbeit *Pongal* hat Funder versucht, die flachen Linienstrukturen eines Kolams ins Dreidimensionale zu überführen. Die gesetzten roten Streifen *(die Gestreiften)* erinnern an die farbliche Gestaltung einiger hinduistischer Heiligtümer, auf die die Künstlerin während ihrer Studienreisen durch Indien, Nepal und Tibet gestoßen ist. Funder geht es hier zudem um das Verhältnis von Fläche und Raum und wie Streifen Einfluss ausüben auf die menschliche Perzeption.

Sowohl in ihrer vegetabilen Formensprache wie auch in den architektonisch anmutenden Strukturen wirken die Objekte Martina Funders äußerlich beruhigt und ausgewogen. Und doch spürt man die intensive innere Kraft, die aus dem Kern der Keramiken nach außen drängt. Die Künstlerin schafft es, auf inhaltlicher wie formaler Ebene das Spannungsverhältnis zwischen ruhender geometrischer Form, der Konstruktion statischer Kompaktheit, organisch-vitalem Bewegungsdrang und gegenständlichem Bezug permanent aufrechtzuerhalten.

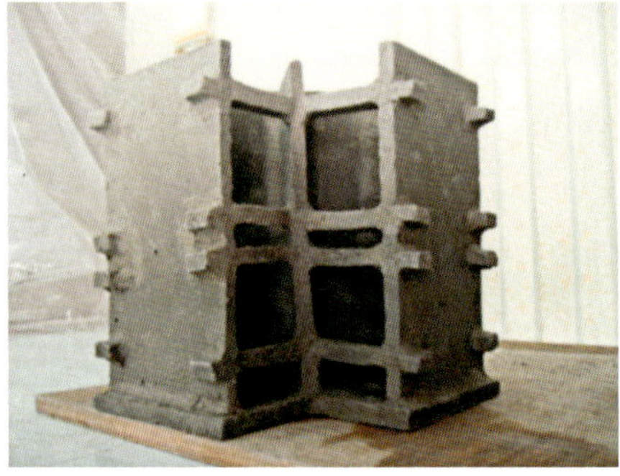

Units aus Korea
2005
3-teilig, Ton
H 60 cm

units from Korea
2005
3-piece, clay
H 60 cm

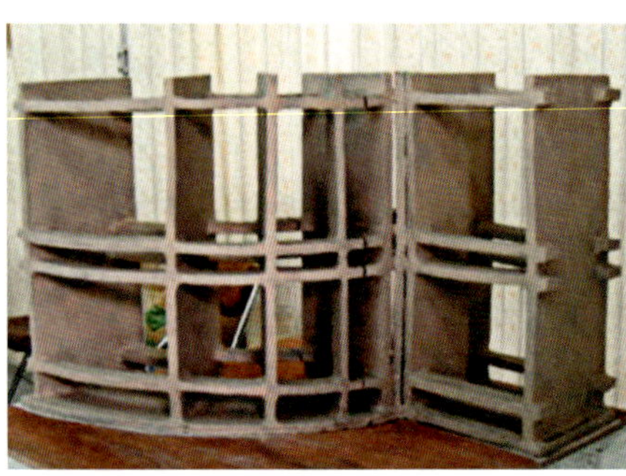

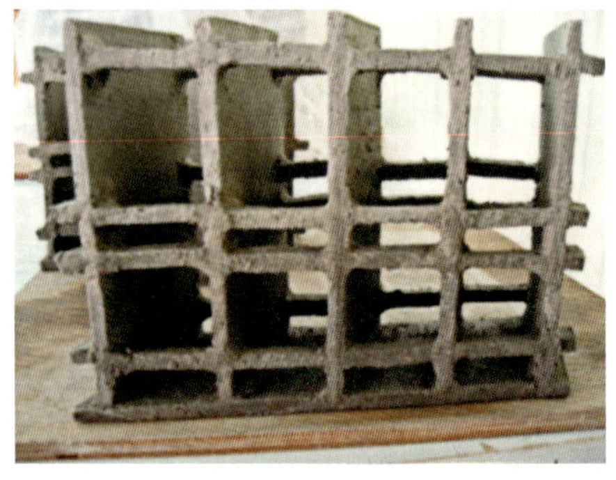

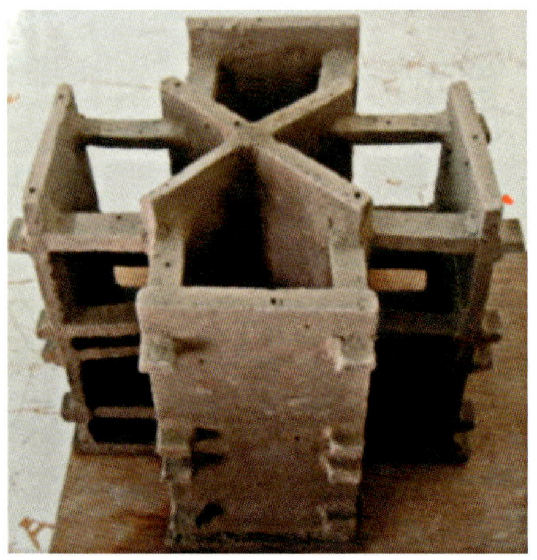

Hartwig Knack

Rhythm – Statics – Construction

Three essential aspects of the ceramic art of Martina Funder

The multi-faceted repertoire of the forms of Martina Funder's ceramics ranges from linear geometric to organic. The surface composition of her objects is raw or rough, smooth or glazed. Nature, with its abundance of patterns, rhythms, and colors, continually provides the artist with new impulses for her art. Still, Funder always weaves into her art current social or political themes which concern or affect her.

Some of her works remind us of modular steel constructions as can be seen in skyscraper architecture; others seem to be abstract likenesses of organic forms. Funder plays with the alleged opposites of organic and geometric, establishing connections and analogies and imposing order. The outcome is art like *Units aus Korea (units from Korea)*, a work that can be viewed as a critical reference to the over two decade long building boom in large parts of Asia. Farmers are being systematically driven from their land and countless migrant workers enslaved. The work *Modul (module) 1-2-3* takes a glance at the regularity and symmetry of a mathematically constructed body and evokes associations of a monumental reinforced concrete skeleton construction, a view that could also be taken from the interior of a biological cell structure.

Martina Funder's objects essentially become accessible at second glance. Her motifs are taken from daily life. She develops her ideas from initially intriguing subjects and found objects. Round flower buds, branches broken off in storms, a log of wood or a dandelion leaf go through transformation processes and shifts in dimensions to become sculptural ceramics with new, haptic qualities and altered levels of content. An example of this is a newspaper article which prompted the artist to critically comment on the excesses of capitalism. In 2001 the Vienna daily newspaper *Der Standard* reported on New Zealand fruit farmers who were about to produce a new variety of kiwi with a red pulp for the global market. Funder spontaneously came up with her works *gelber Kiwiziegel (yellow kiwi brick)* and *globalisierte Kiwis (globalized kiwis)* in the shades of yellow, bronze, red, dark red, dark green, as well as matt black, and glossy black. The artist ironized the strategies of the advertising industry by presenting an expanded range of colors as a provocative innovation. In this way Funder satirized one of the primary characteristics of capitalism: maximizing profit through the development of supposedly new goods.

In all cultures the line is a symbol of life, a mirror of speed, but also a metaphor of tranquility and rationality. Humankind's earliest artistic expressions were expressed in a linear fashion: just think of the cave paintings of prehistoric times. As children we all drew stick figures when we began to scribble our first experiences on paper. The line, the foundation of every human made shape, is also prevalent in many of Martina Funder's works. Sometimes the artist uses nature as a model, as in the work *panorama*, where she let herself be inspired by the mood of a ridge of hills in a foggy haze against the backdrop of the rising sun.

In other works, she applies her line to symmetrical patterns and structures as in a Tamil Kolam, a sketch that women in the South of India draw and regularly renew at their doorsteps to keep away bad sprits. In the work *Pongal*, Funder tries to make the flat line structure of a kolam three-dimensional. The positioned red stripes of *die Gestreiften (the striped)* are reminiscent of the colorful compositions of some Hindi shrines which the artists had the opportunity to experience first hand when she travelled as a student through India, Nepal, and Tibet. Here Funder is concerned with the relationship between surface and space, and the influence stripes have on human perception.

In her organic form language or in the architecture-like structures, Martina Funder's objects come across as externally calm and well balanced. And yet, we still feel the intense inner power that surges out of the core of her ceramic art. On the level of form as well as content, the artist always manages to sustain the balance between geometric forms at rest, the construction of static compactness, and representational reference together with the organic, vital urge of movement.

3 Putzschwämme
2006
gebrannter, eingefärbter und glasierter Ton
à 2,5 x 10 x 6 cm

3 cleaning sponges
2006
fired, colored, and glazed clay
2.5 x 10 x 6 cm each

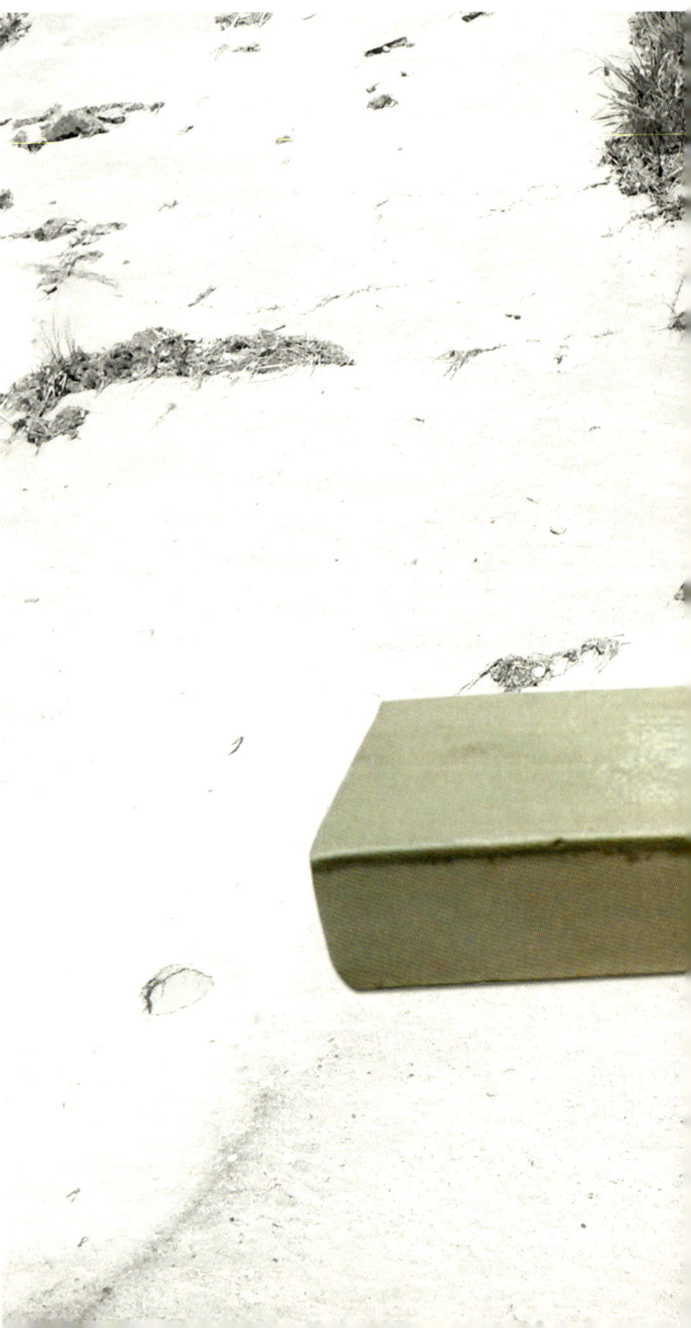

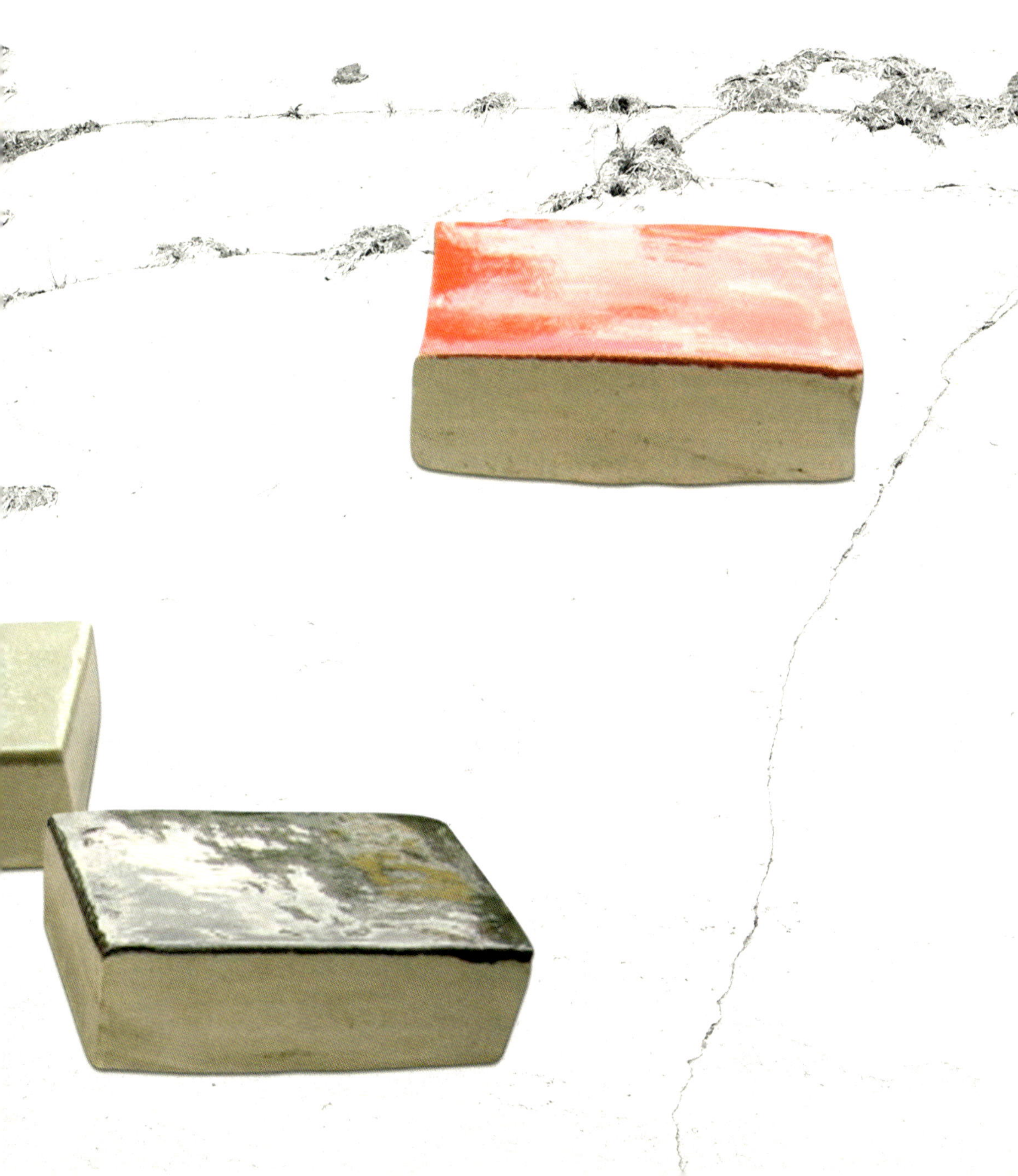

die Gefallenen
2006
6 Stück, gebrannter und glasierter Ton
größtes Stück 1,5 x 39 x 32 cm

the fallen
2006
6 pieces, fired and glazed clay
biggest piece 1.5 x 39 x 32 cm

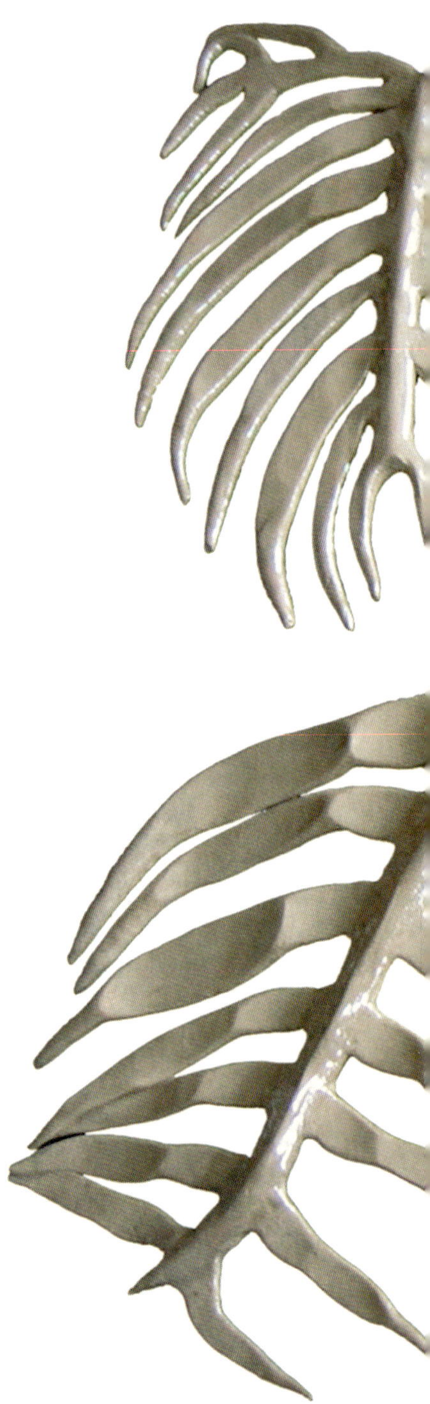

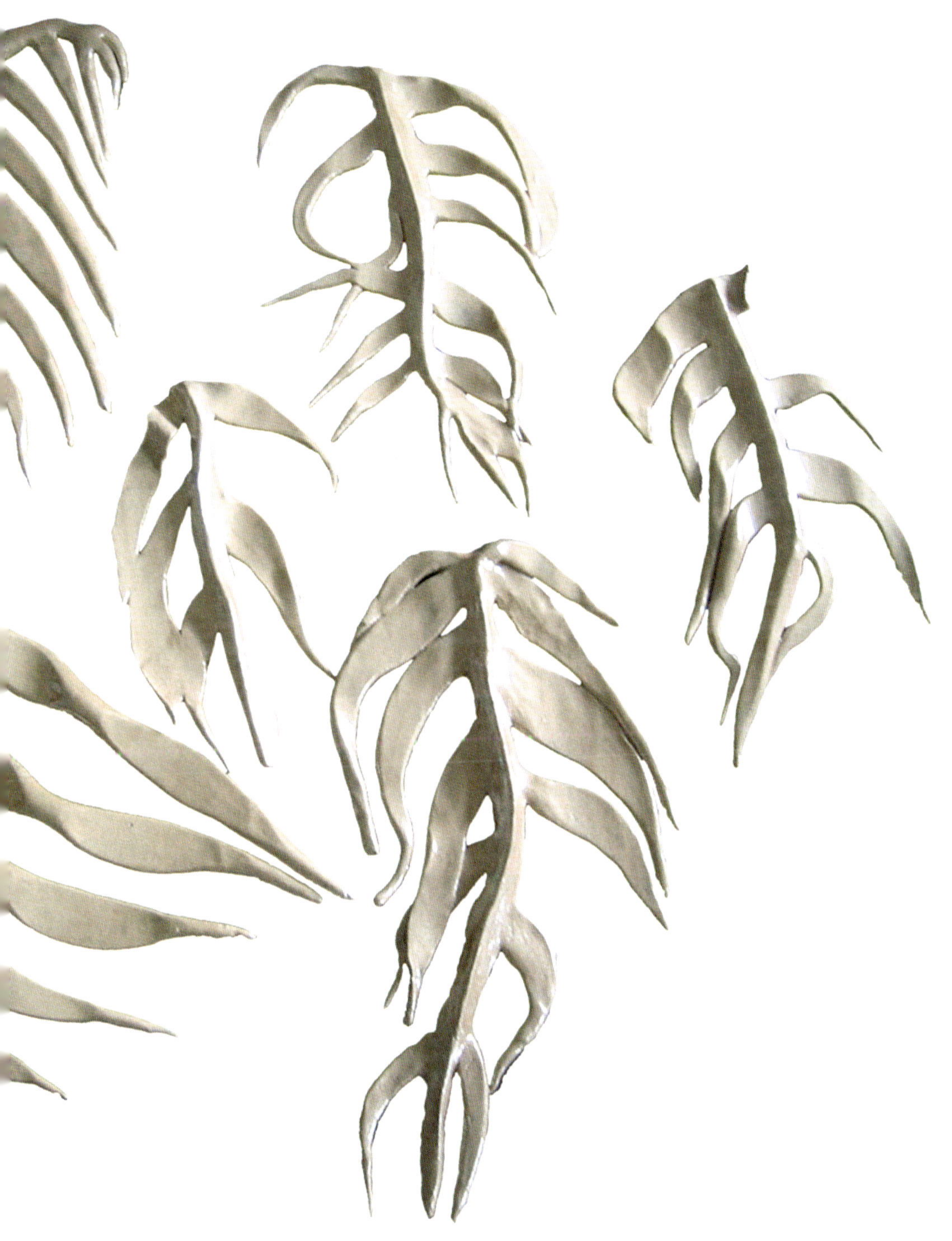

donnerstags
2010
Bleistift auf Papier
70 x 50 cm

Thursdays
2010
pencil on paper
70 x 50 cm

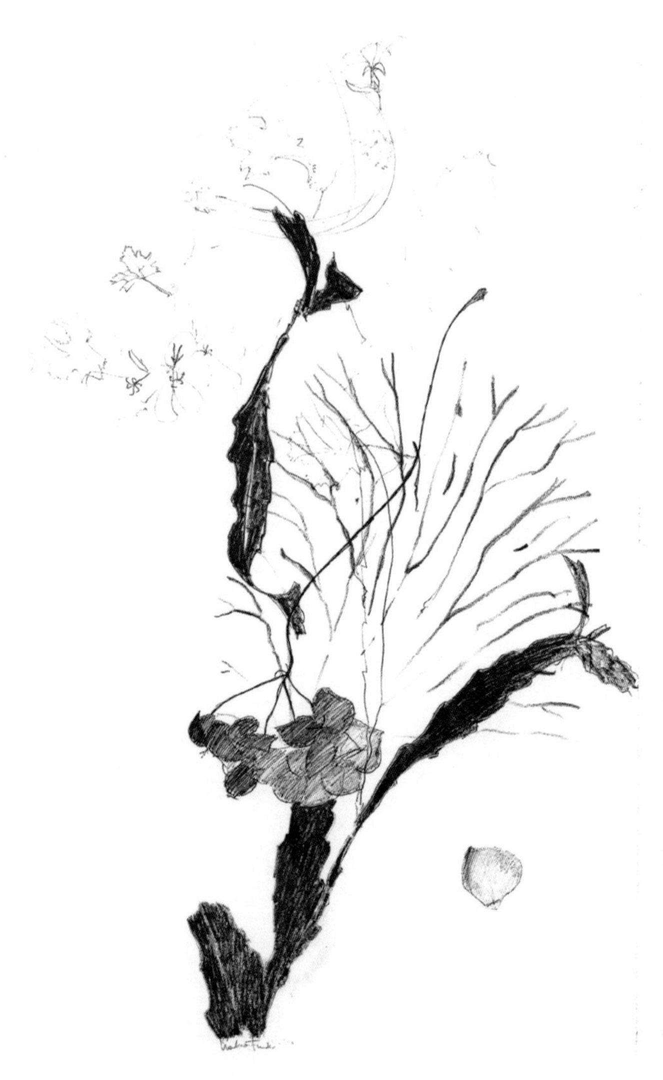

freitags
2010
Bleistift auf Papier
70 x 50 cm

Fridays
2010
pencil on paper
70 x 50 cm

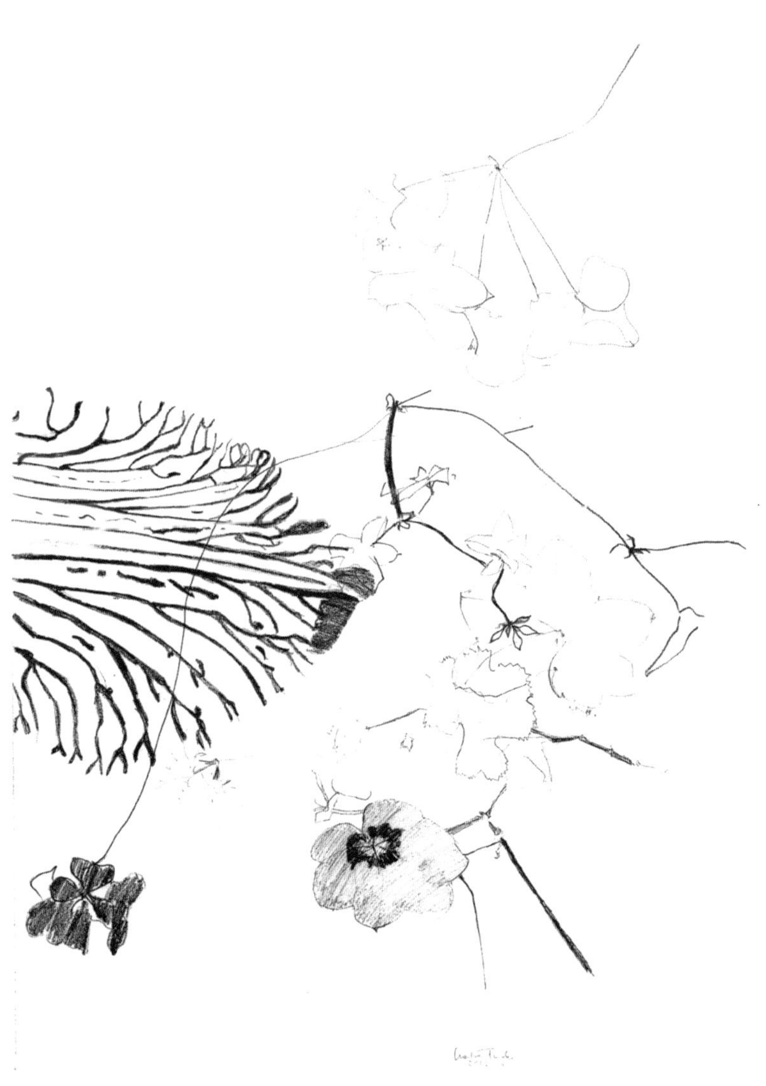

Cortex
2006
gebrannter und glasierter Ton
3 x 28 x 13 cm

cortex
2006
fired and glazed clay
3 x 28 x 13 cm

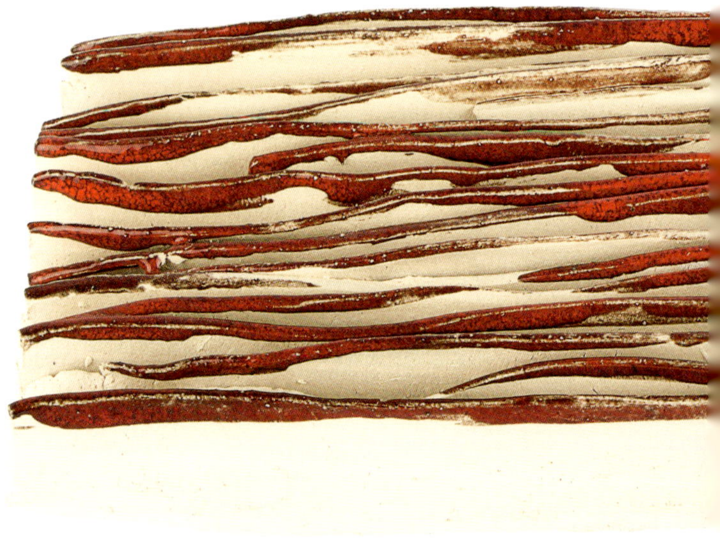

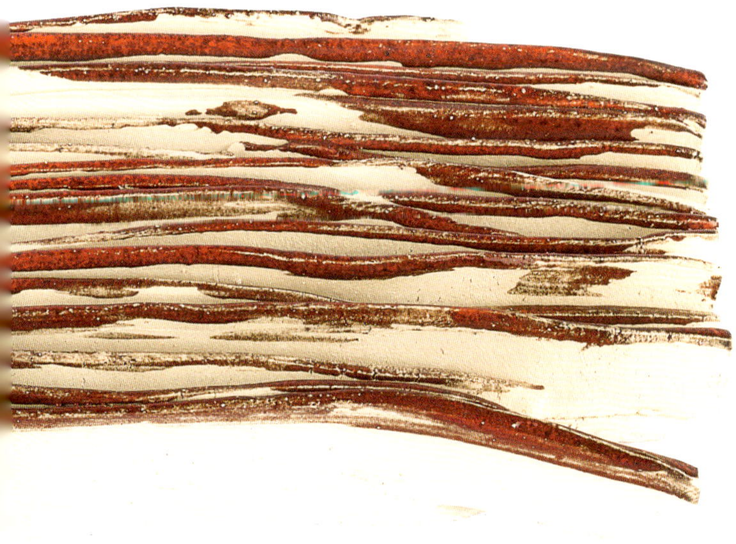

Modul 1-2-3
2007
3-teilig, gebrannter und glasierter Ton
60 x 90 x 30 cm

module 1-2-3
2007
3-piece, fired and glazed clay
60 x 90 x 30 cm

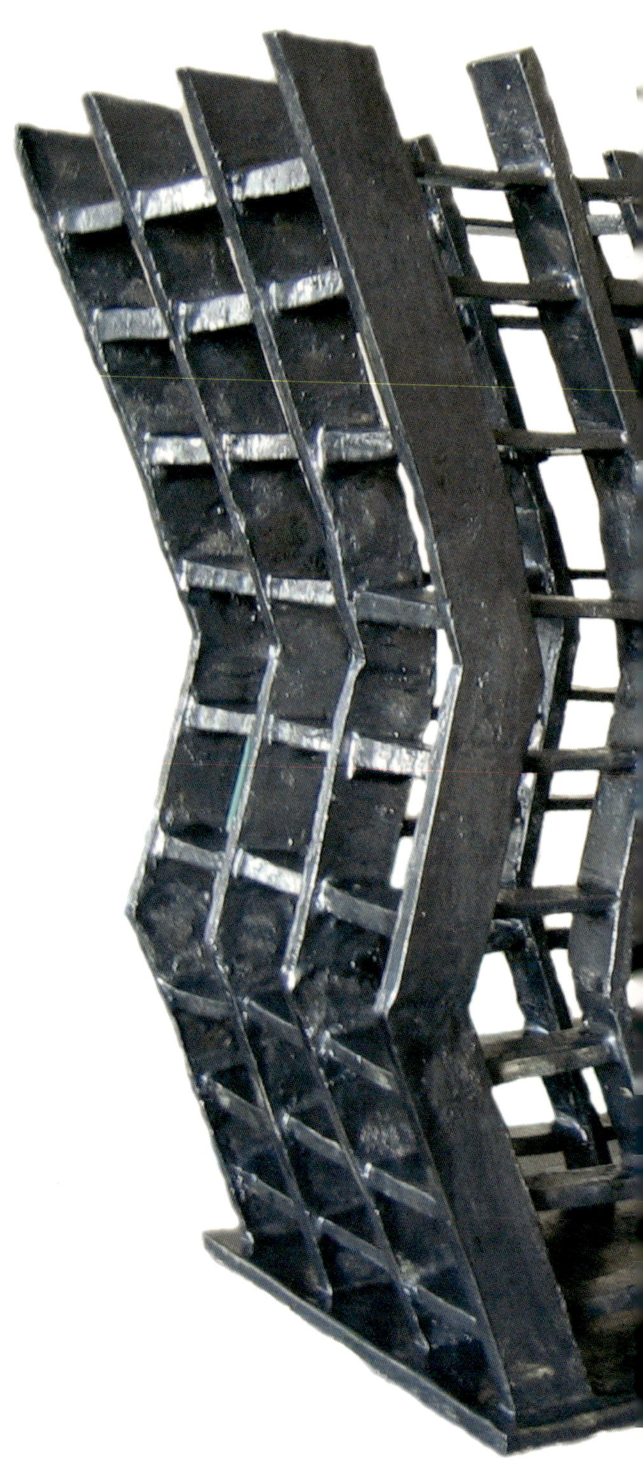

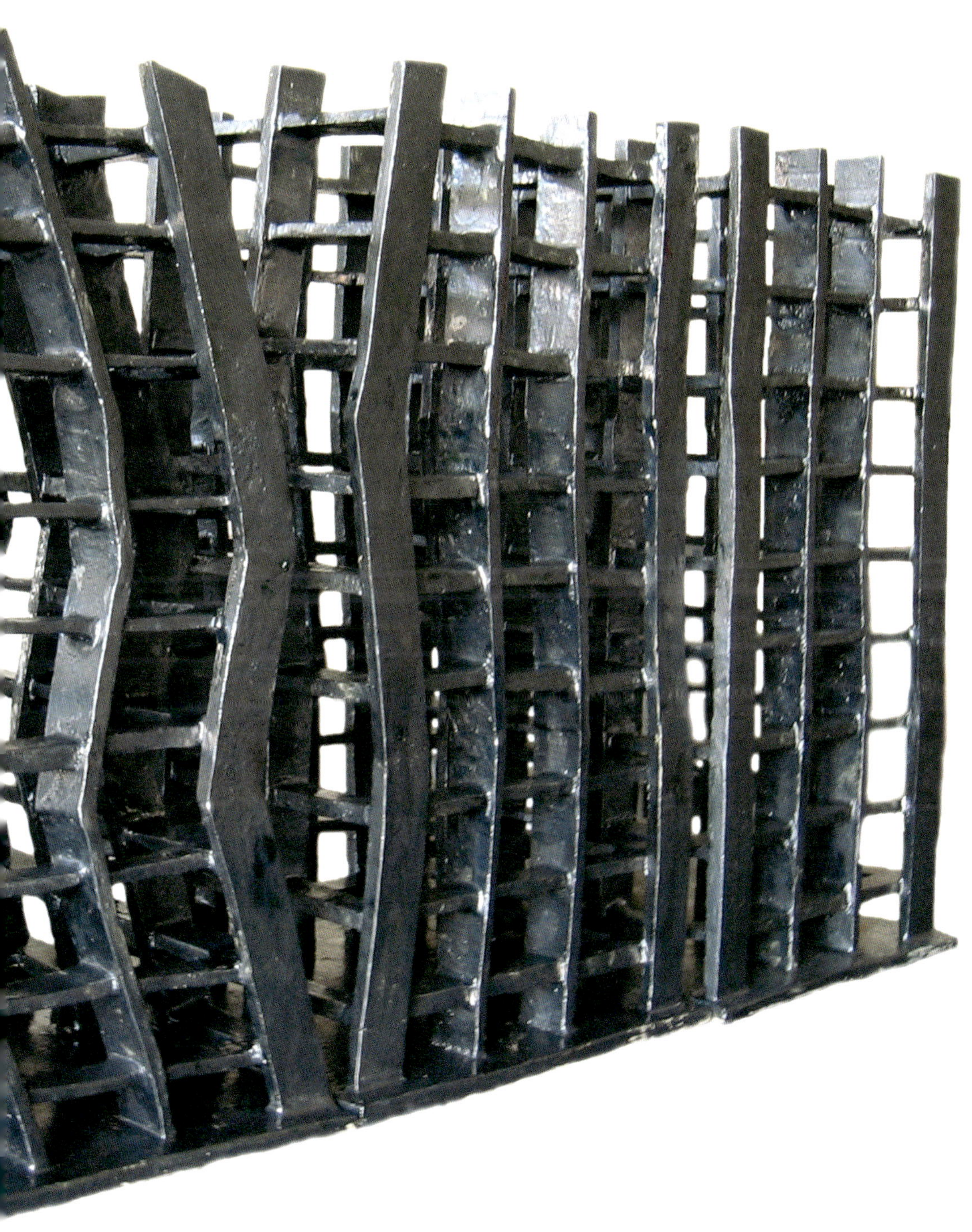

gefaltet
2010
Bleistift auf Papier
100 x 70 cm

folded
2010
pencil on paper
100 x 70 cm

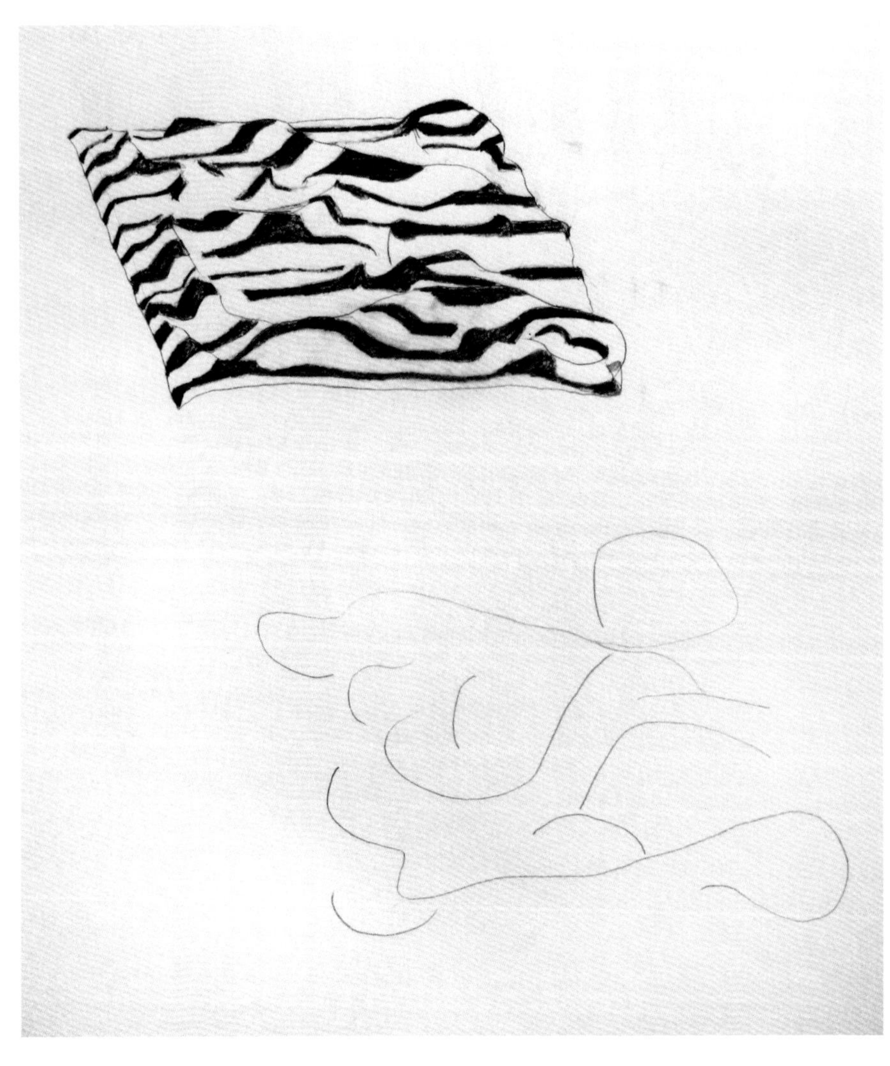

die Gestreiften
2009
2 Stück, gebrannter und engobierter Ton
5 x 28 x 26 cm, 3 x 28 x 28 cm

the striped
2009
2 pieces, fired and engobed clay
5 x 28 x 26 cm, 3 x 28 x 28 cm

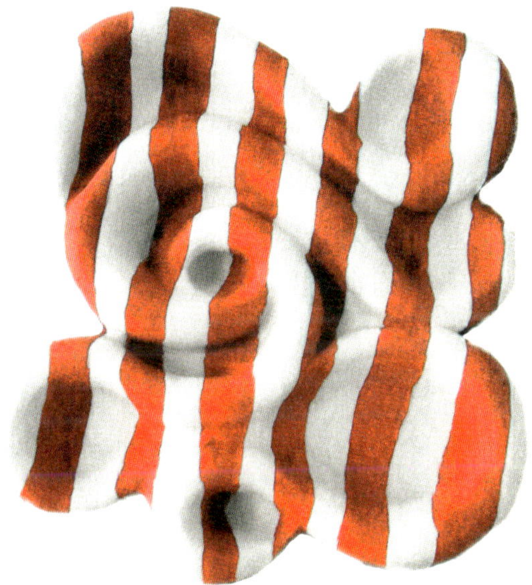

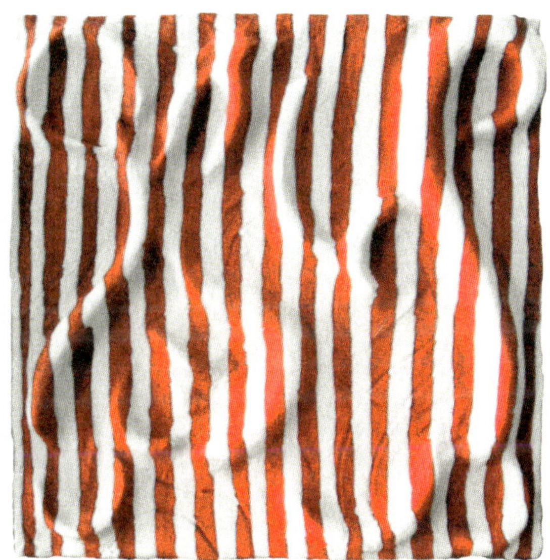

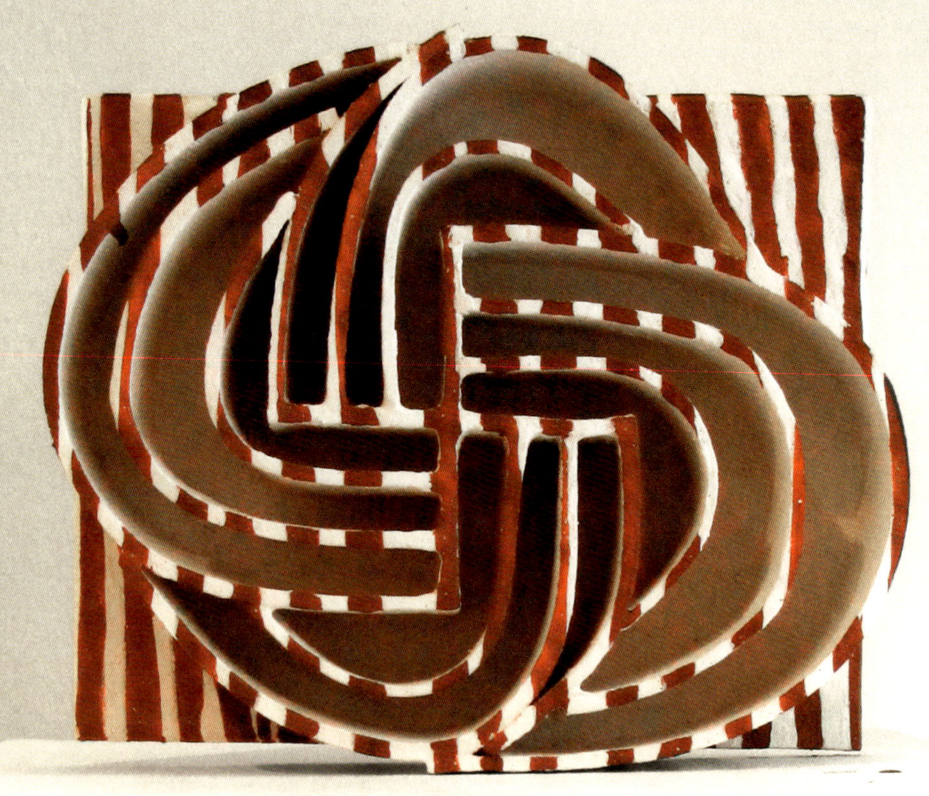

Pongal 1
2009
gebrannter und engobierter Ton
6,5 x 27 x 23 cm

Pongal 1
2009
fired and engobed clay
6.5 x 27 x 23 cm

Pongal 2
2009
gebrannter und engobierter Ton
6,5 x 27 x 23 cm

Pongal 2
2009
fired and engobed clay
6.5 x 27 x 23 cm

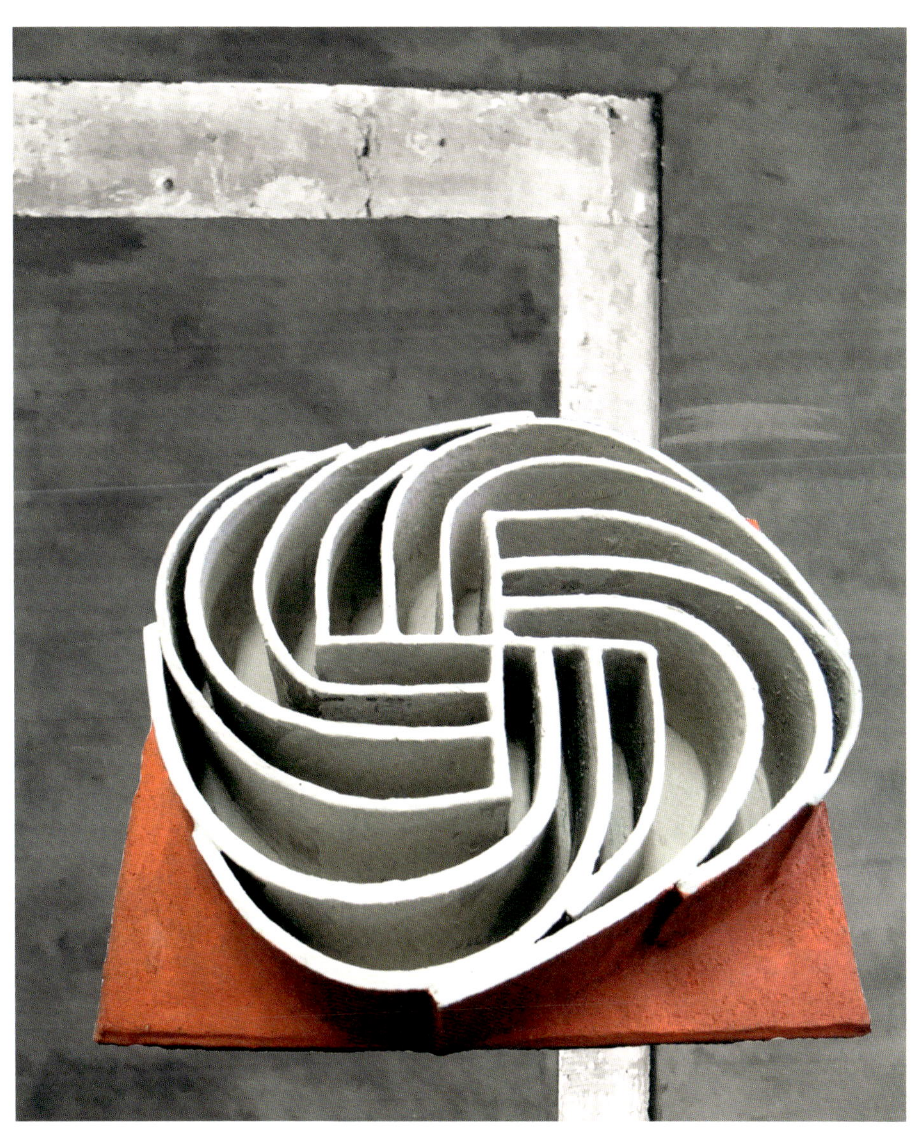

Pongal ersetzt
2009
Bleistift auf Papier
44 x 63 cm

Pongal replaced
2009
pencil on paper
44 x 63 cm

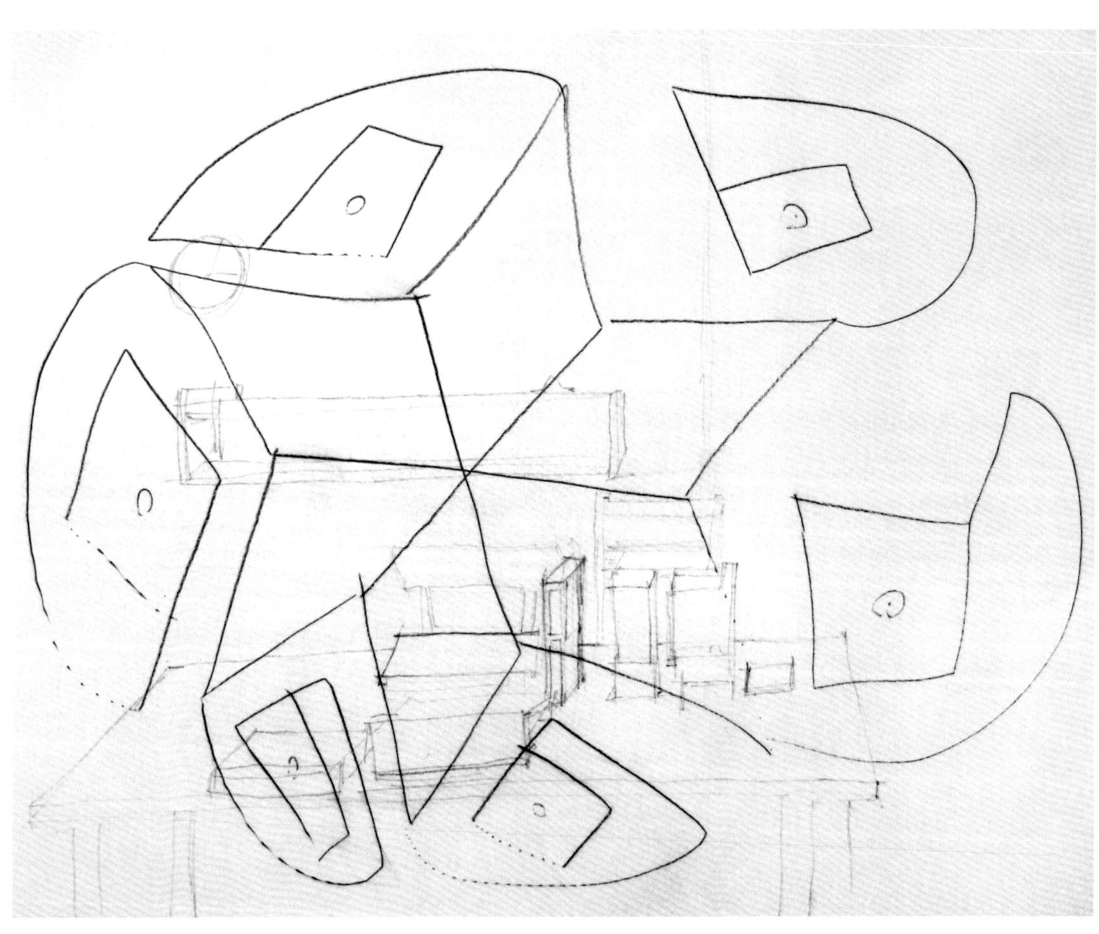

Pongal wiederhergestellt
2009
Bleistift auf Papier
44 x 63 cm

Pongal restored
2009
pencil on paper
44 x 63 cm

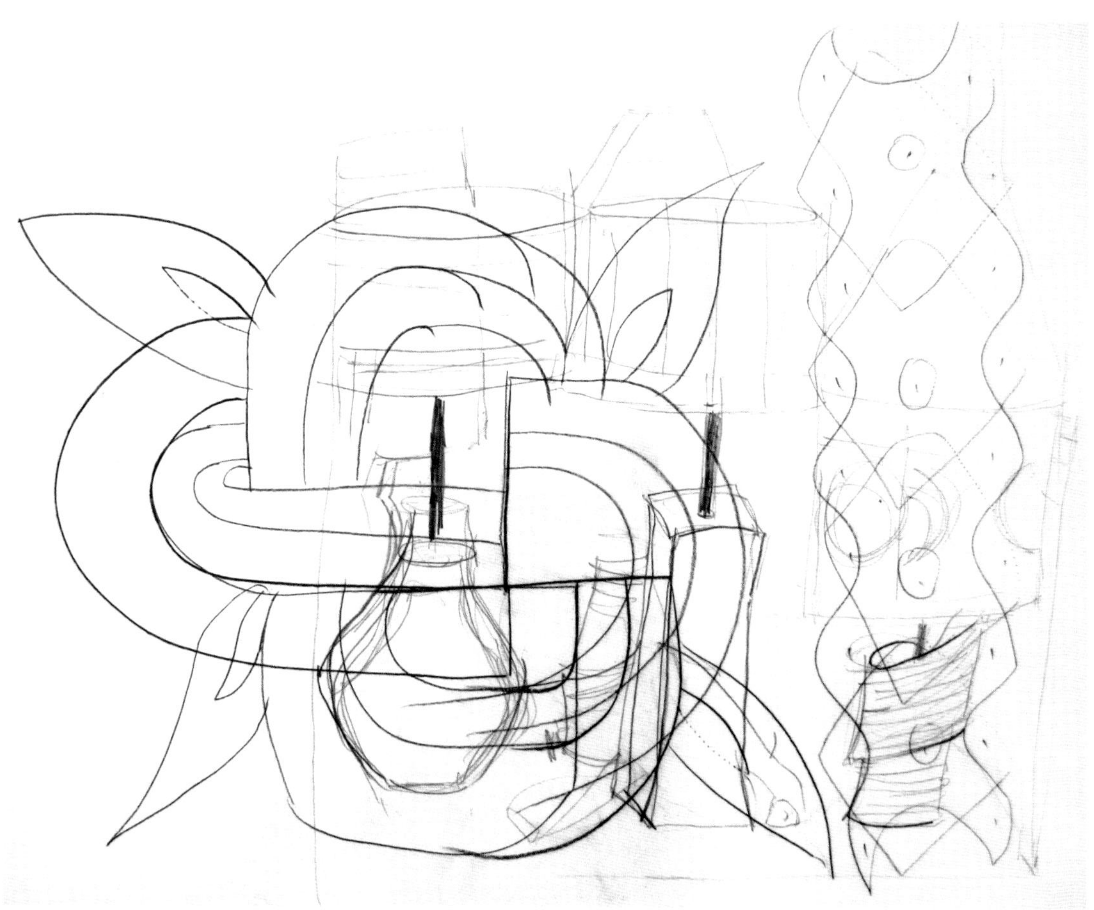

Cut 1 und Cut 2
2010
gebrannter und glasierter Ton
H 17 cm, D 12 cm
H 17 cm, D 9 cm

cut 1 and cut 2
2010
fired and glazed clay
H 17 cm, D 12 cm
H 17 cm, D 9 cm

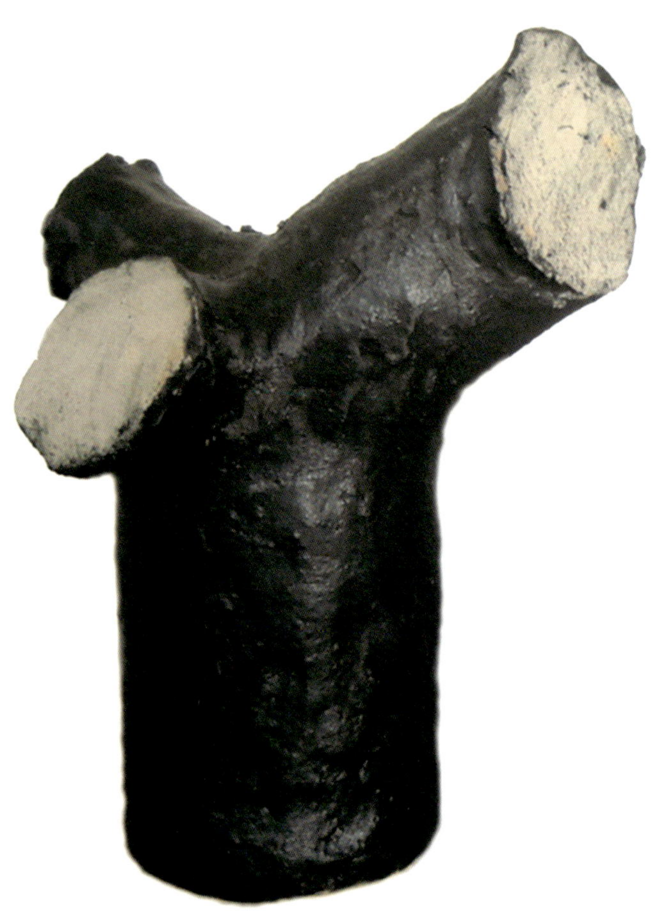

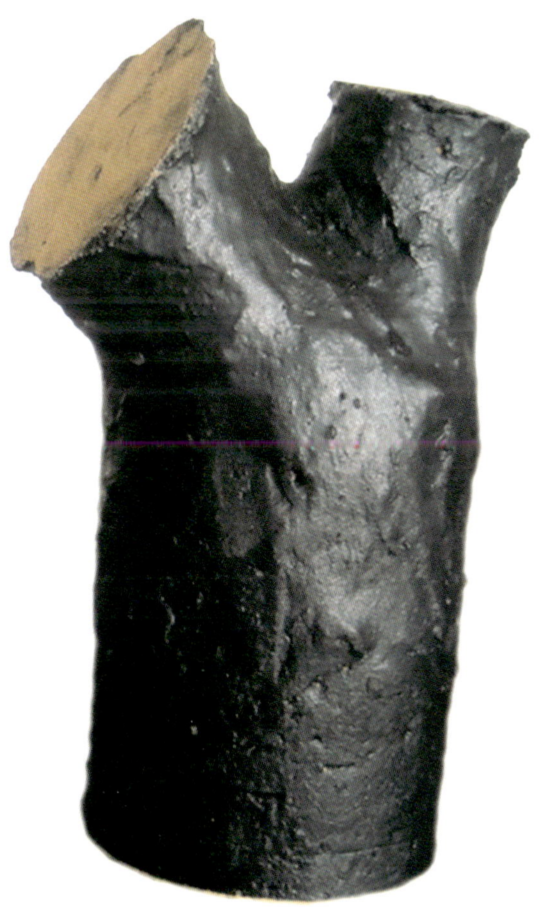

Blatt und sein Gerippe
2010
2-teilig, gebrannter und glasierter Ton
6 x 58 x 25 cm, 1 x 58 x 25 cm

leaf and its skeleton
2010
2-piece, fired and glazed clay
6 x 58 x 25 cm, 1 x 58 x 25 cm

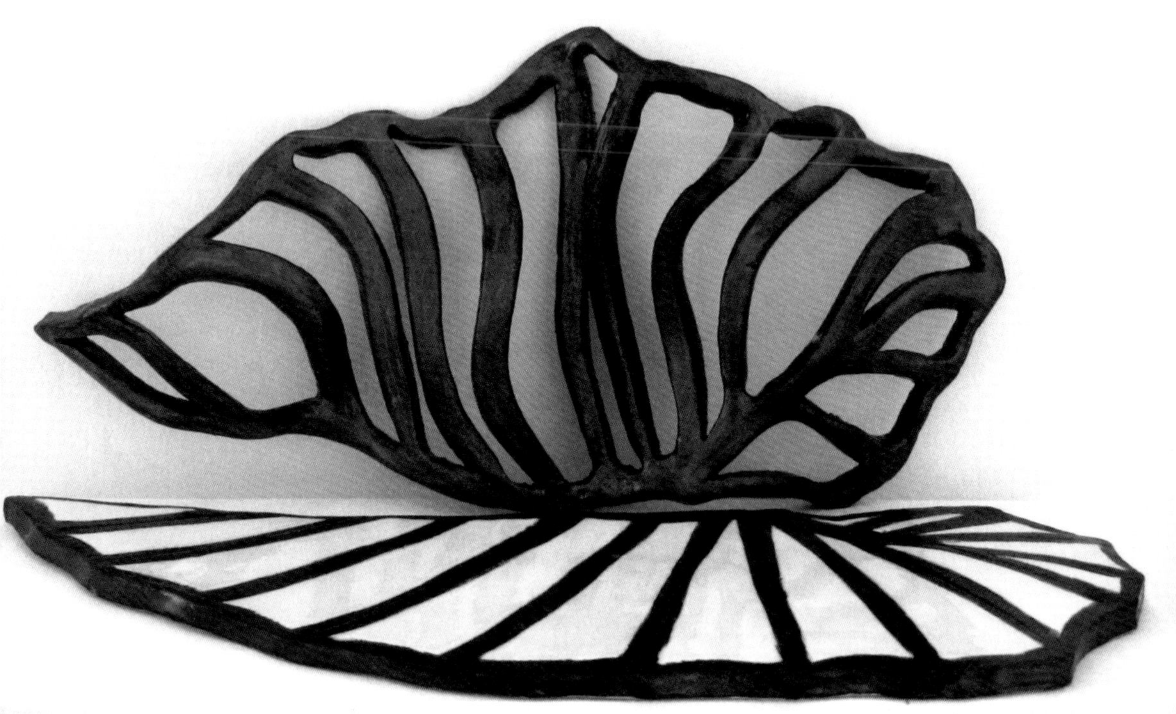

gelber Wischer
2010
gebrannter und engobierter Ton
5 x 32 x 32 cm

yellow wiper
2010
fired and engobed clay
5 x 32 x 32 cm

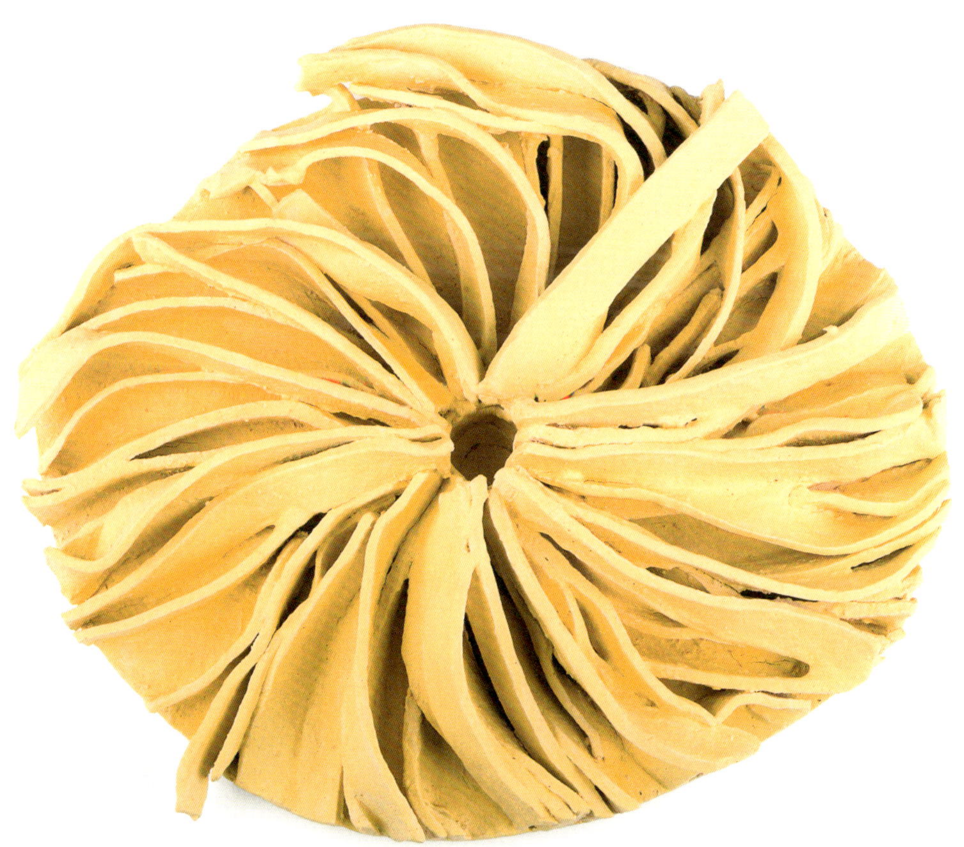

Panorama – Teil von 7
2010
gebrannter, engobierter und glasierter Ton
9 x 59 x 23 cm

panorama – part of 7
2010
fired, engobed, and glazed clay
9 x 59 x 23 cm

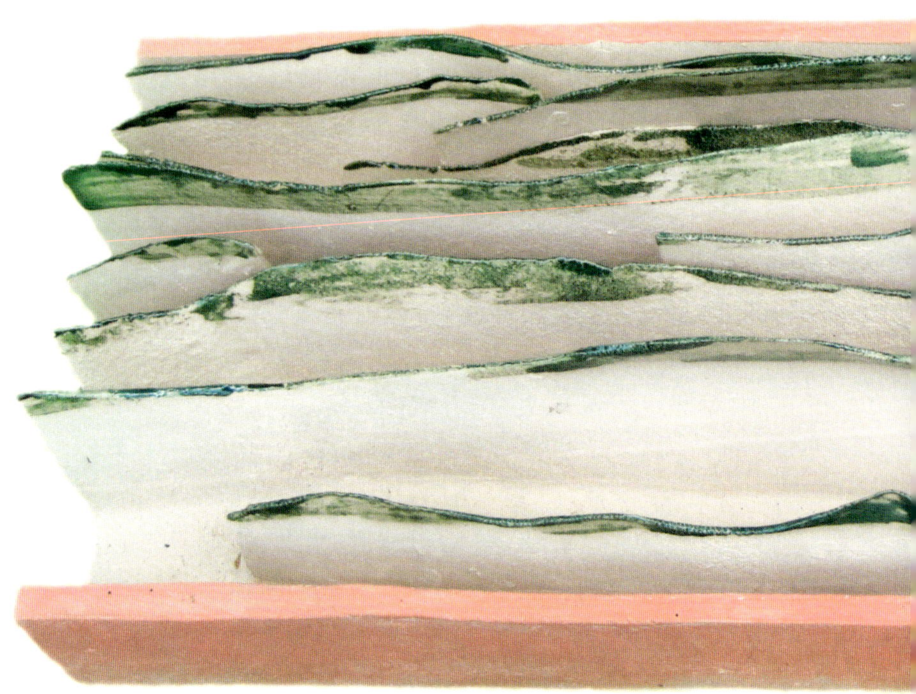

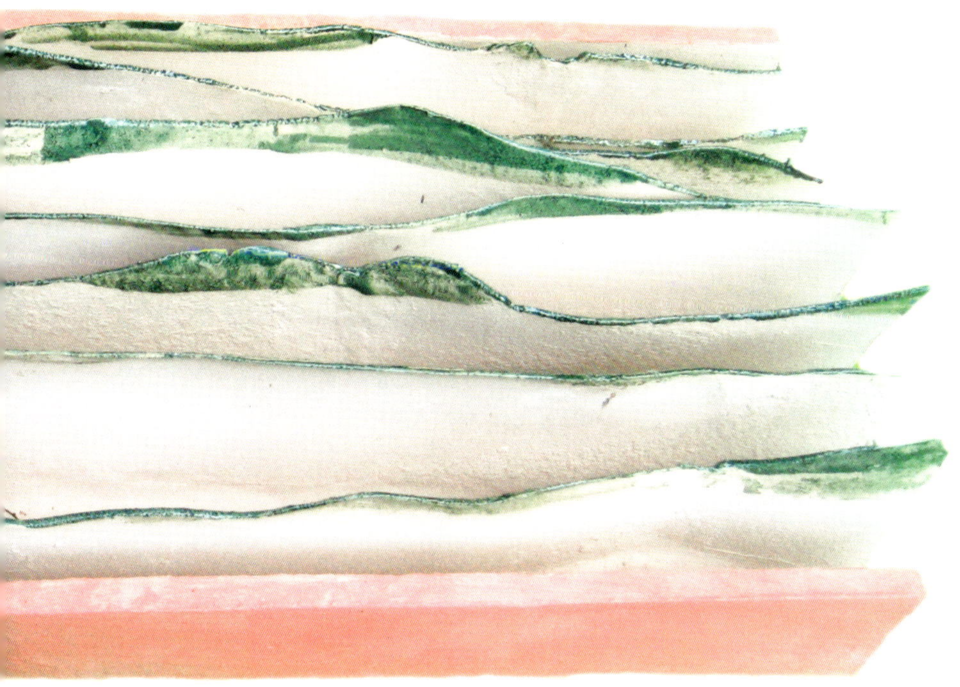

rote Furchen
2011
gebrannter und glasierter Ton
8 x 48 x 30 cm

red grooves
2011
fired and glazed clay
8 x 48 x 30 cm

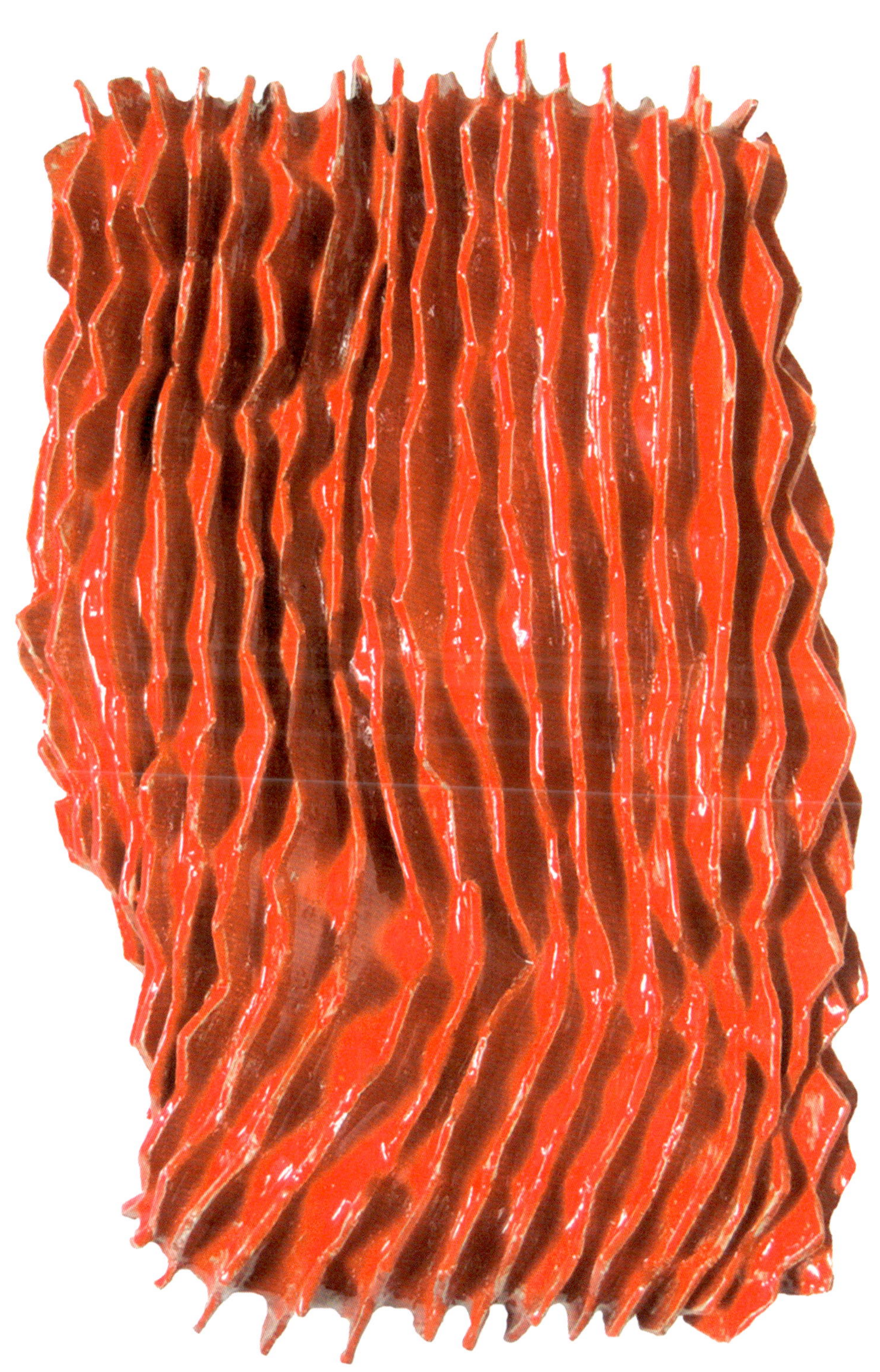

Inkamauer
2014
5-teilig, gebrannter Ton mit Oxyden eingefärbt
4,5 x 149 x 34 cm

Inca wall
2014
5-piece, fired clay colored with oxide
4.5 x 149 x 34 cm

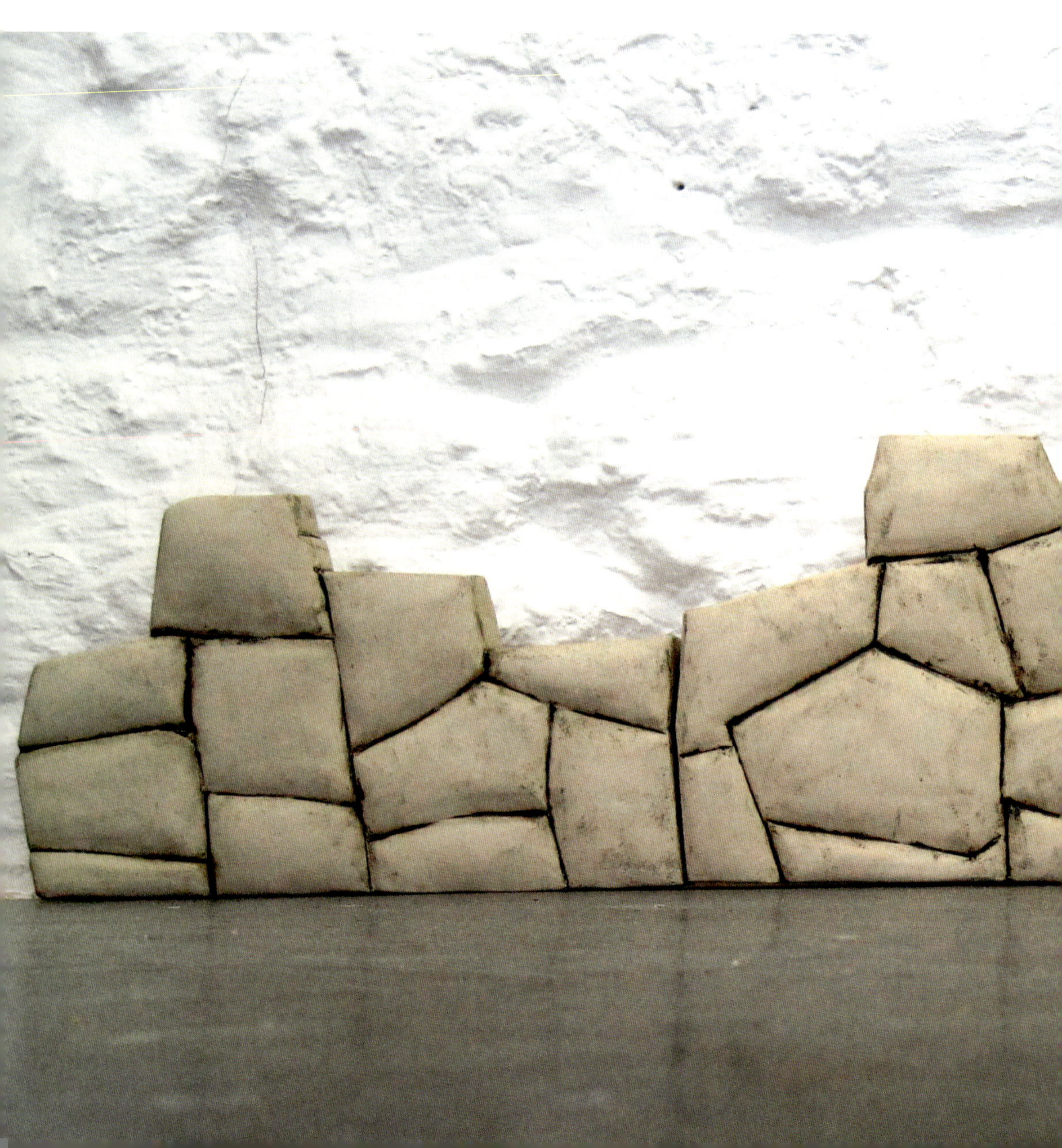

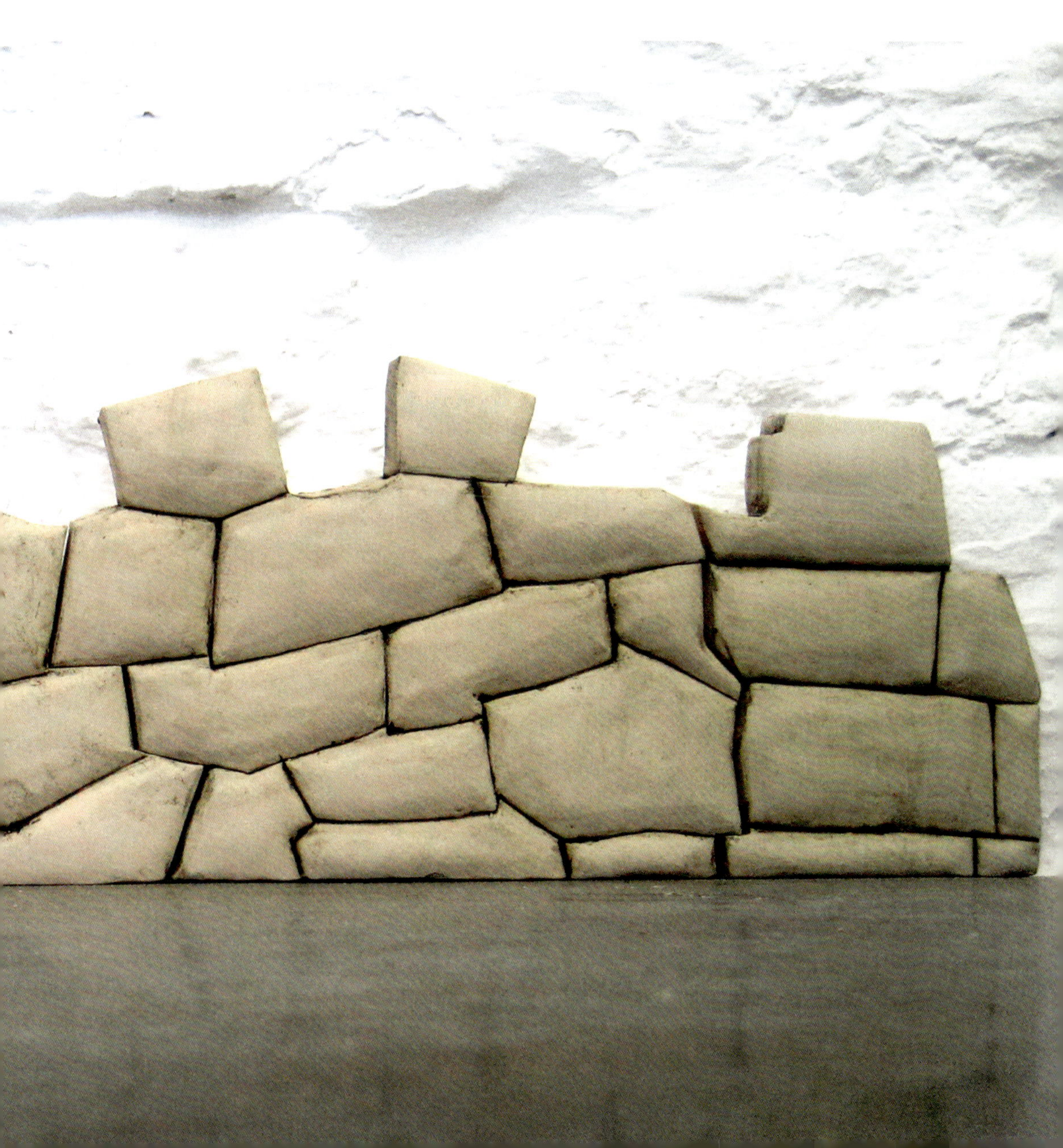

Inkamauer 2
2014
Bleistift auf Papier
30 x 50 cm

Inca wall 2
2014
pencil on paper
30 x 50 cm

Inkamauer 3
2014
Bleistift auf Papier
30 x 50 cm

Inca wall 3
2014
pencil on paper
30 x 50 cm

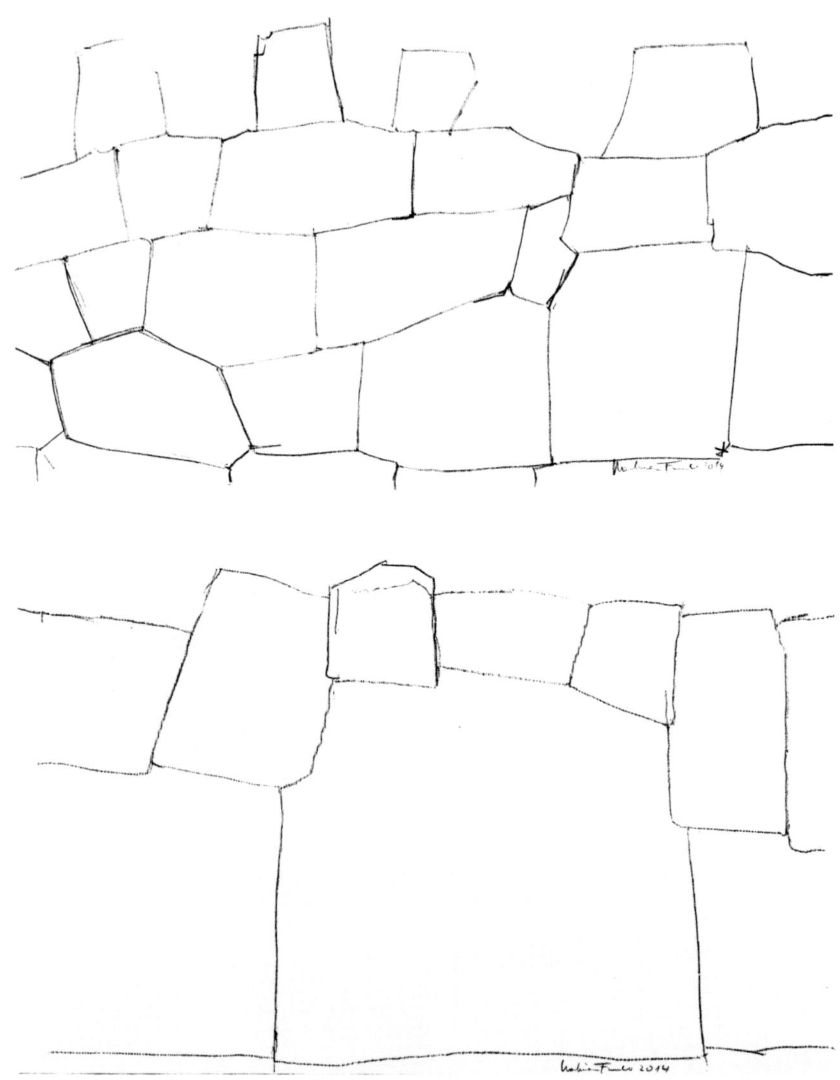

Mauerstück
2014
gebrannter und glasierter Ton
14 x 28 x 7,5 cm

piece of wall
2014
fired and glazed clay
14 x 28 x 7.5 cm

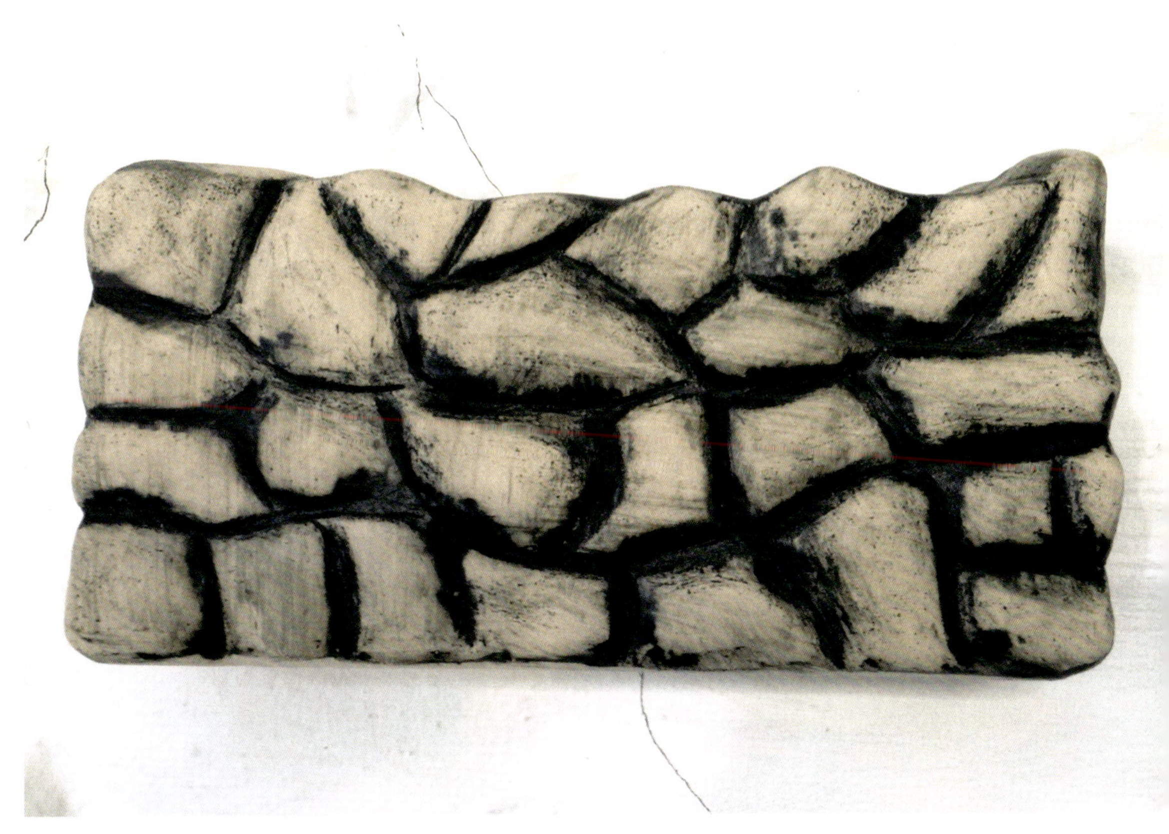

Inkamatratze
2014
27-teilig, gebrannter und glasierter Ton
mit 1 textilen Teil
7 x 166 x 74 cm

Inca mattress
2014
27-piece, fired and glazed clay
with 1 part textile
7 x 166 x 74 cm

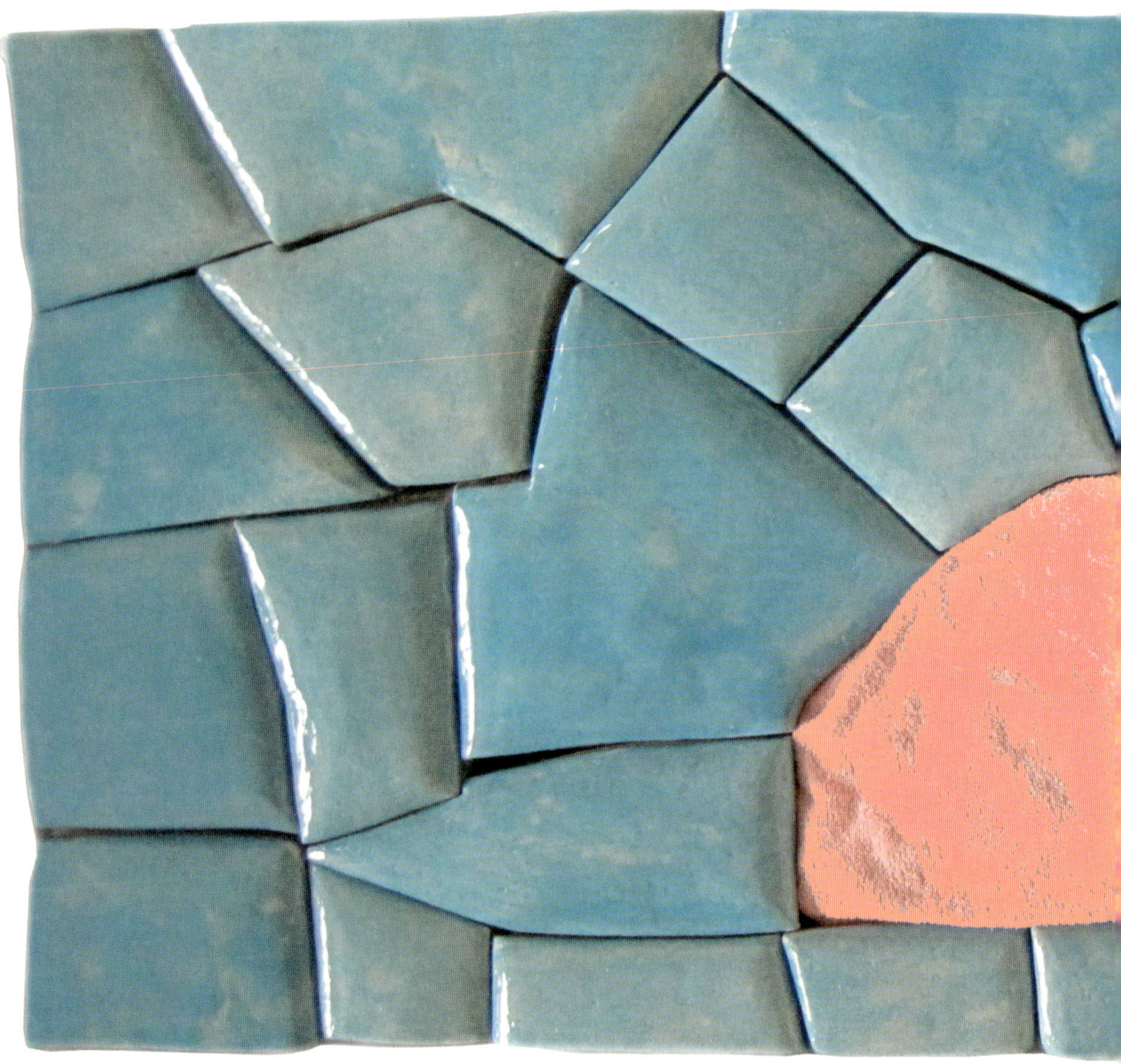

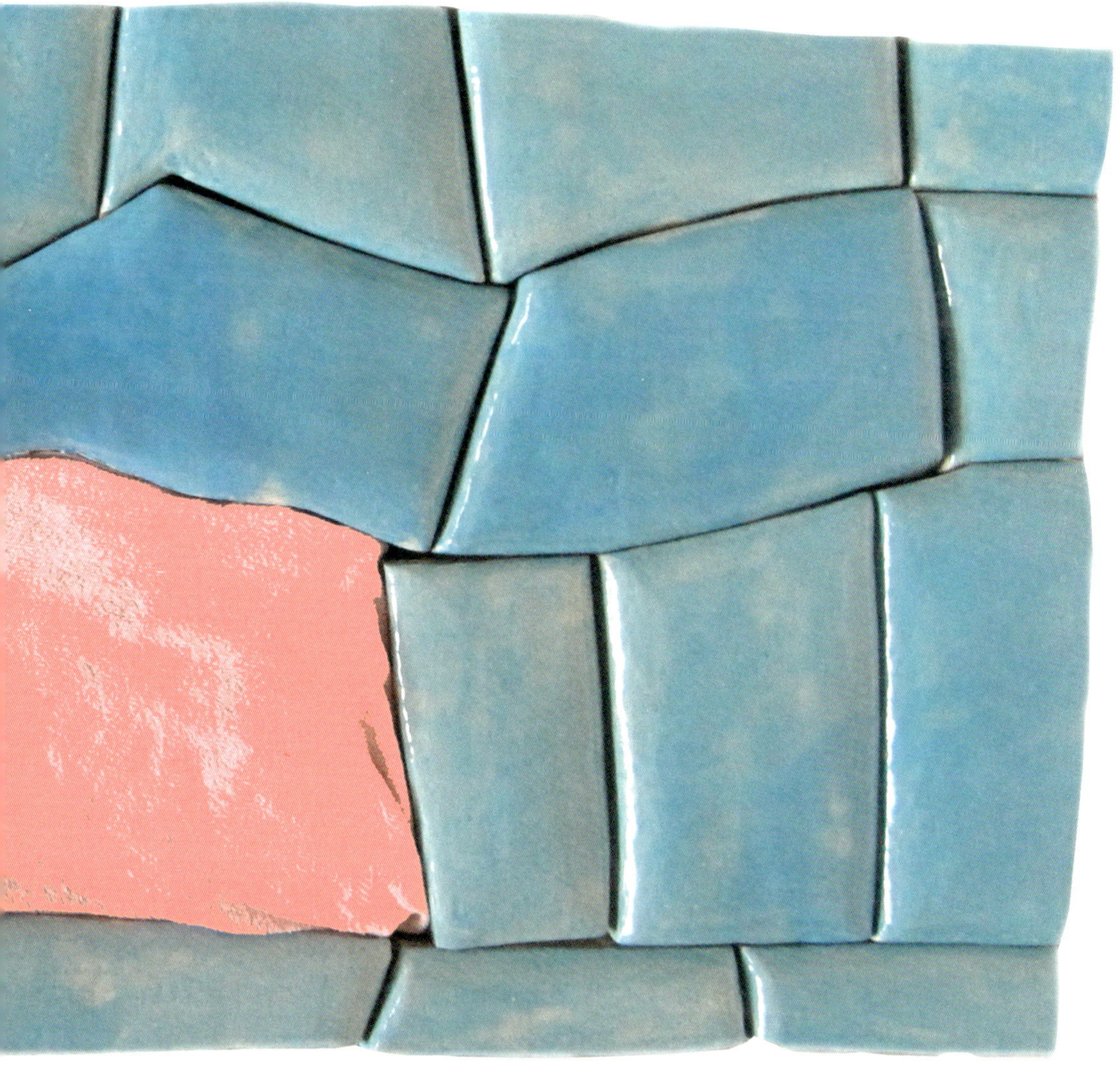

Berg der Steinböcke
2015
gebrannter, glasierter und vergoldeter Ton
12 x 24 x 14 cm

mountain of ibexes
2015
fired, glazed, and gold-plated clay
12 x 24 x 14 cm

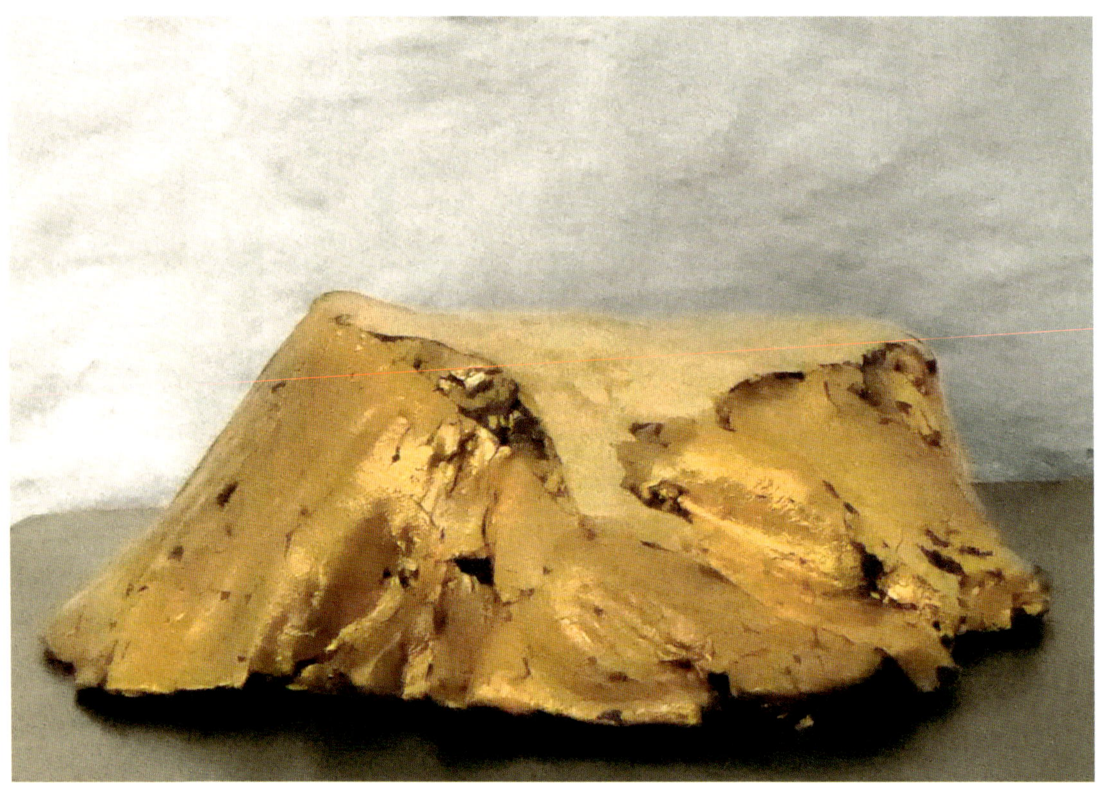

Gipfel des Altaigebirges
2015
gebrannter, glasierter und vergoldeter Ton
11 x 20 x 6 cm

summits of the Altai mountains
2015
fired, glazed, and gold-plated clay
11 x 20 x 6 cm

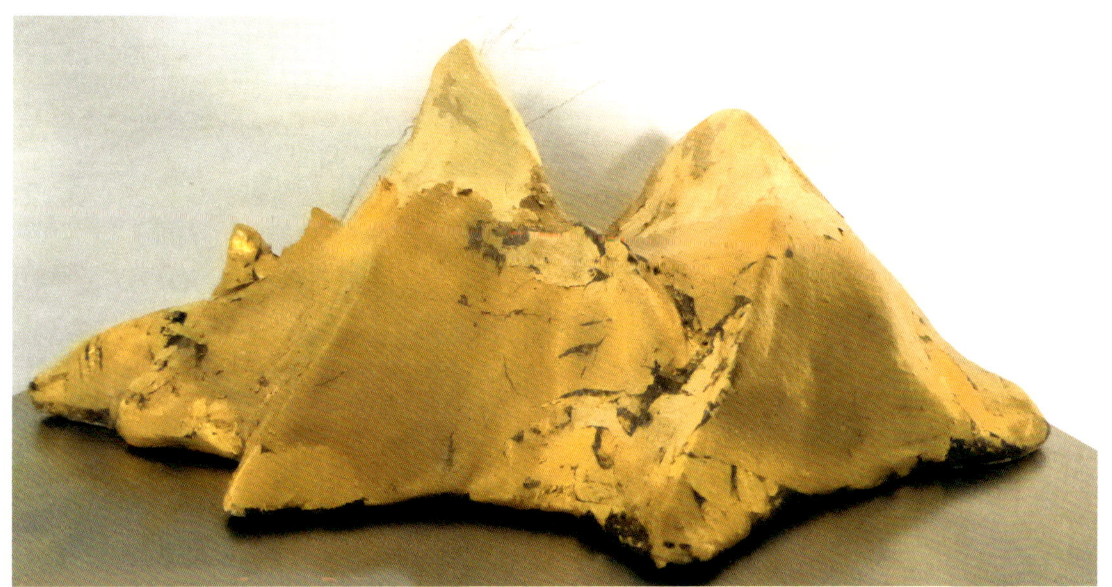

Gurla Mandata 3
2011
Bleistift auf Papier
10 x 15 cm

Gurla Mandata 3
2011
pencil on paper
10 x 15 cm

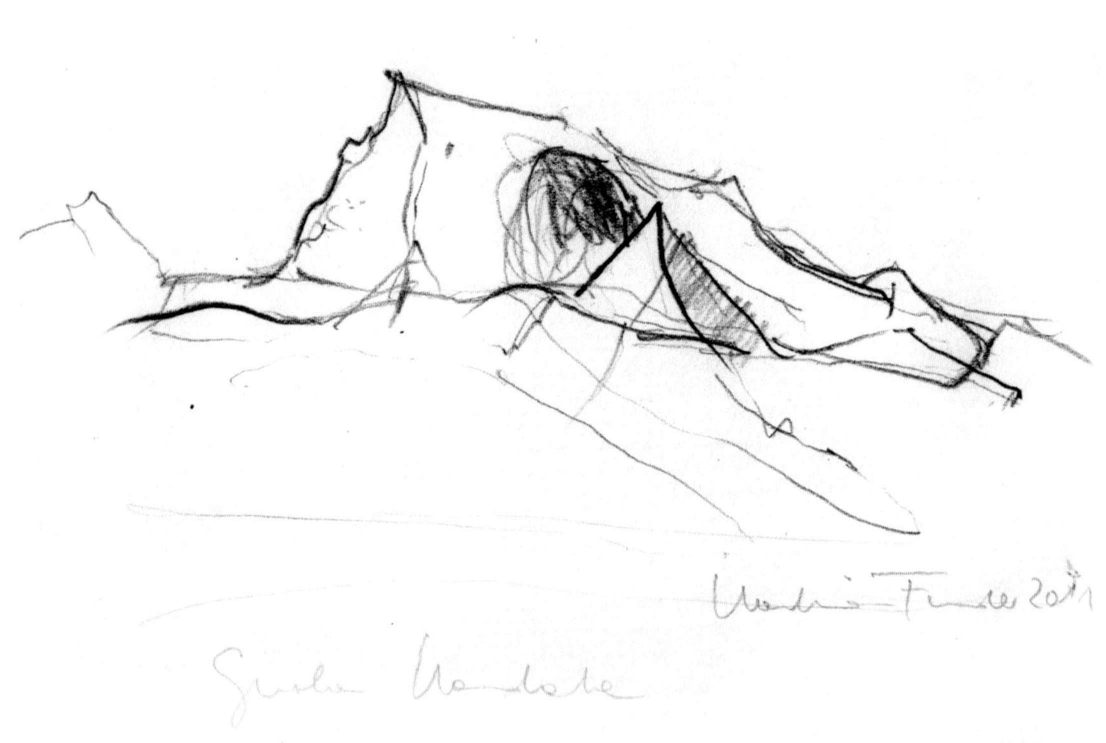

Kailash 2
2011
Bleistift auf Papier
10 x 15 cm

Kailash 2
2011
pencil on paper
10 x 15 cm

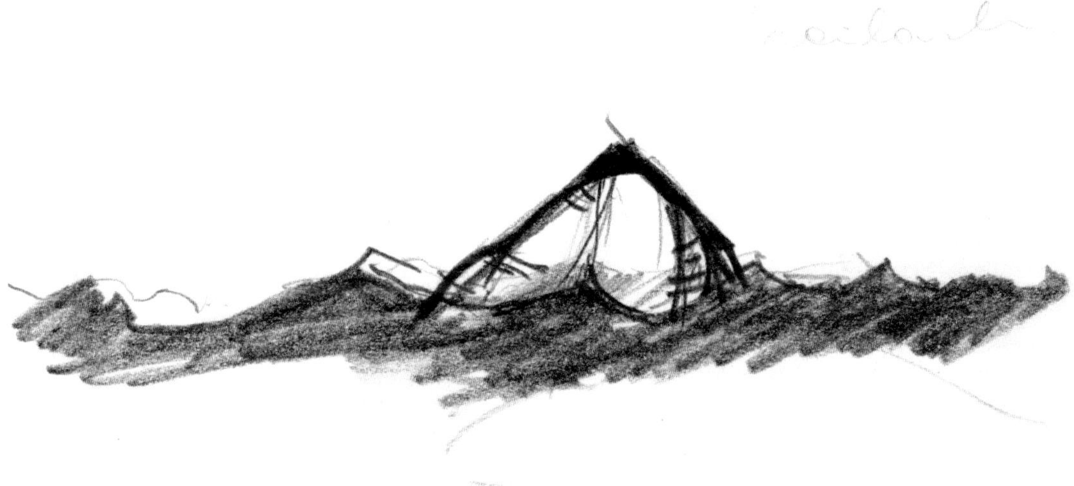

schwarze Kornjaca
2016
gebrannter und glasierter Ton
3 x 32 x 31 cm

black kornjaca
2016
fired and glazed clay
3 x 32 x 31 cm

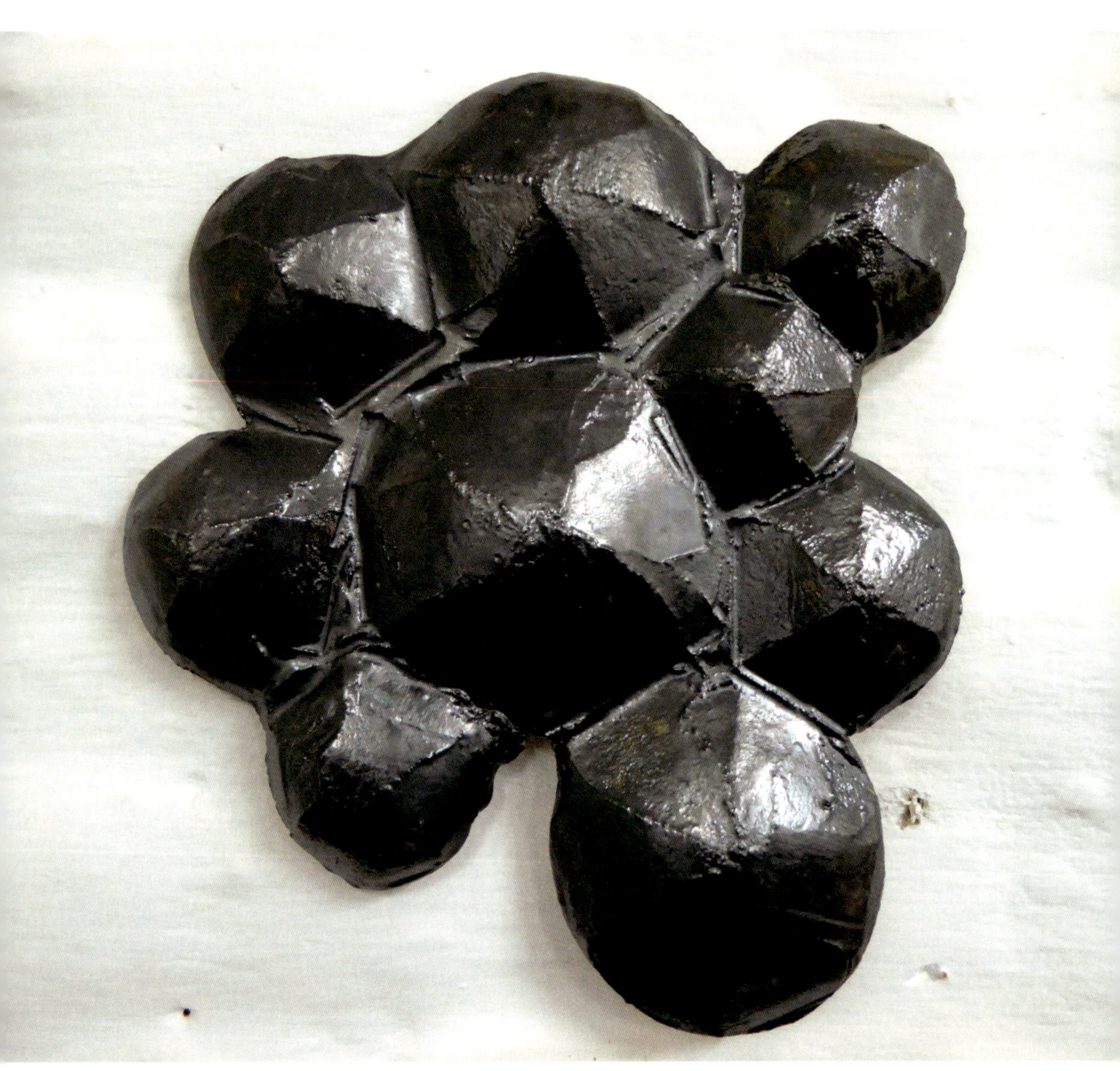

Kornjaca im Winter
2016
gebrannter und glasierter Ton
3 x 39 x 30 cm

kornjaca in winter
2016
fired and glazed clay
3 x 39 x 30 cm

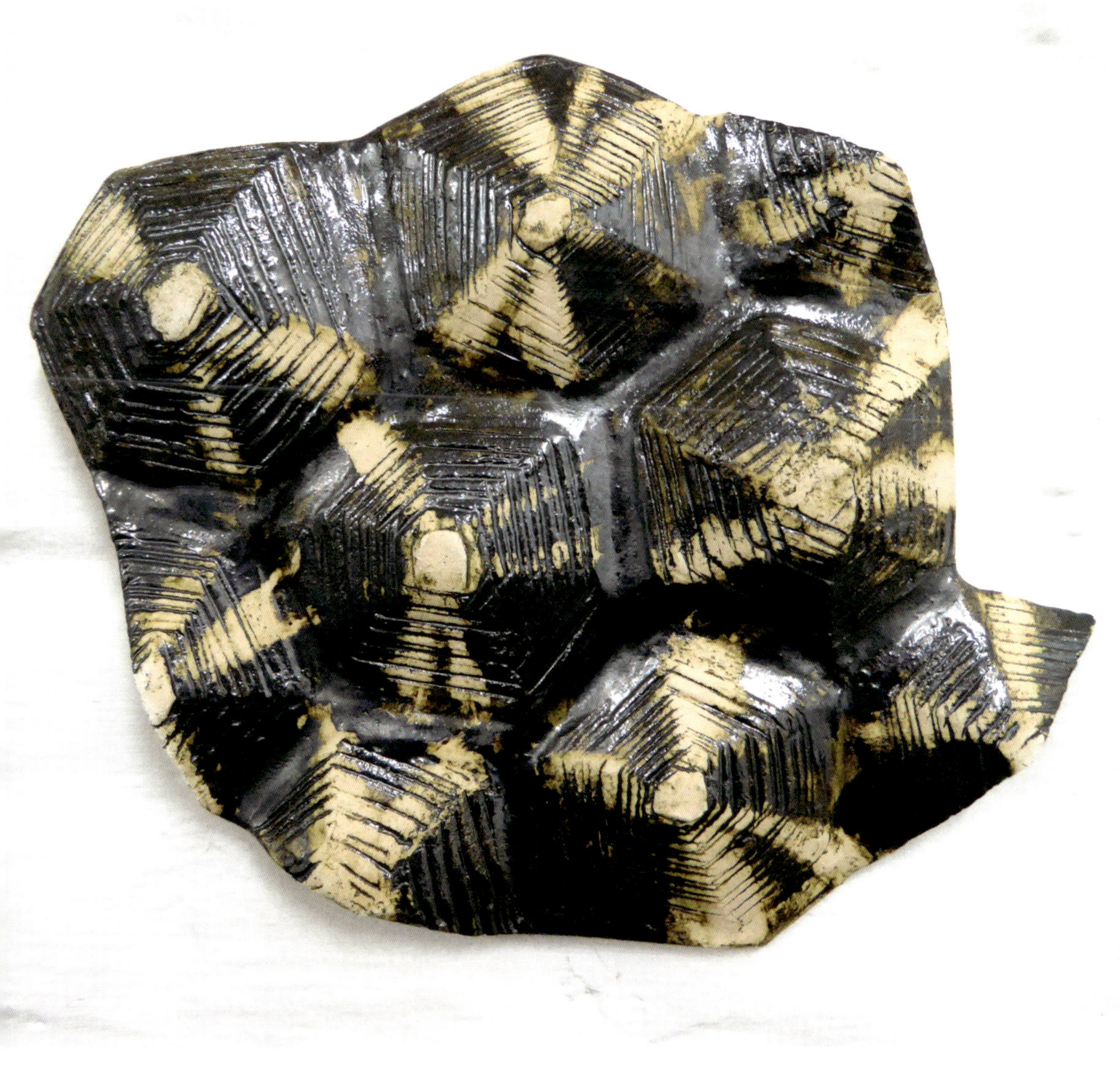

karnisch 3
2012
Bleistift auf Papier
21 x 30 cm

carnic 3
2012
pencil on paper
21 x 30 cm

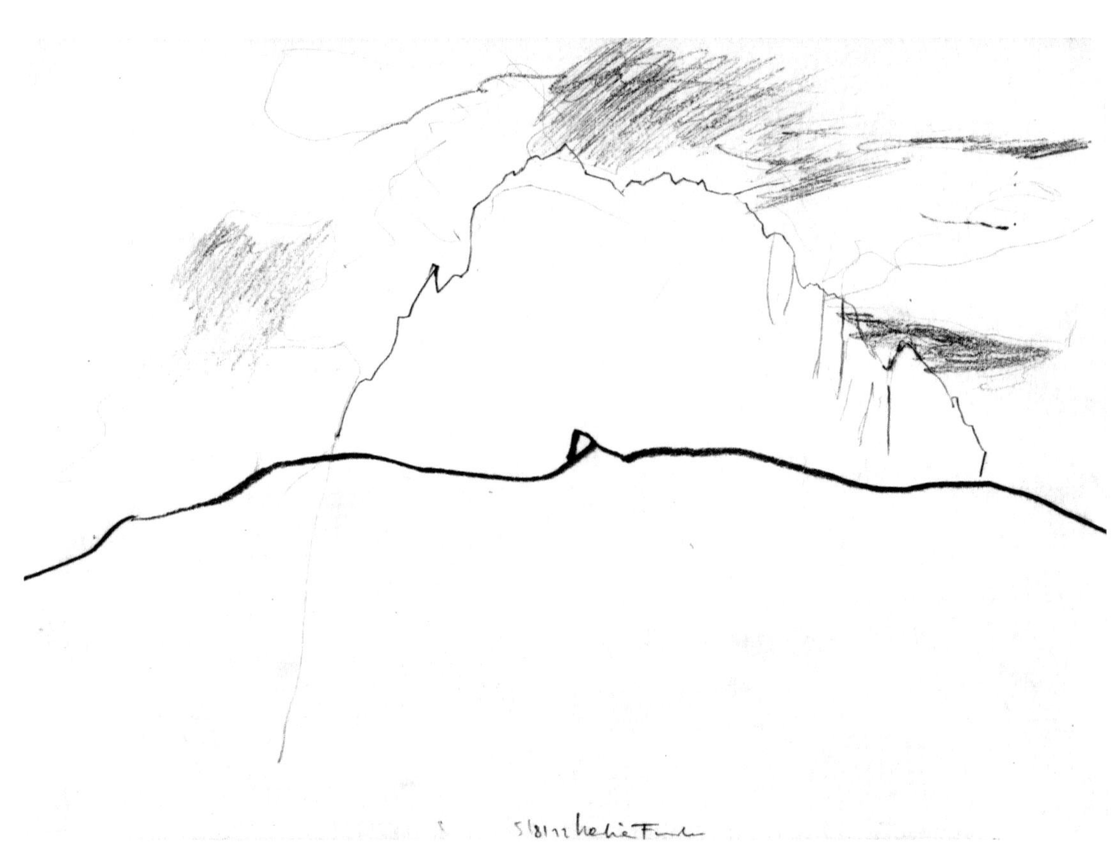

karnisch 4
2012
Bleistift auf Papier
21 x 30 cm

carnic 4
2012
pencil on paper
21 x 30 cm

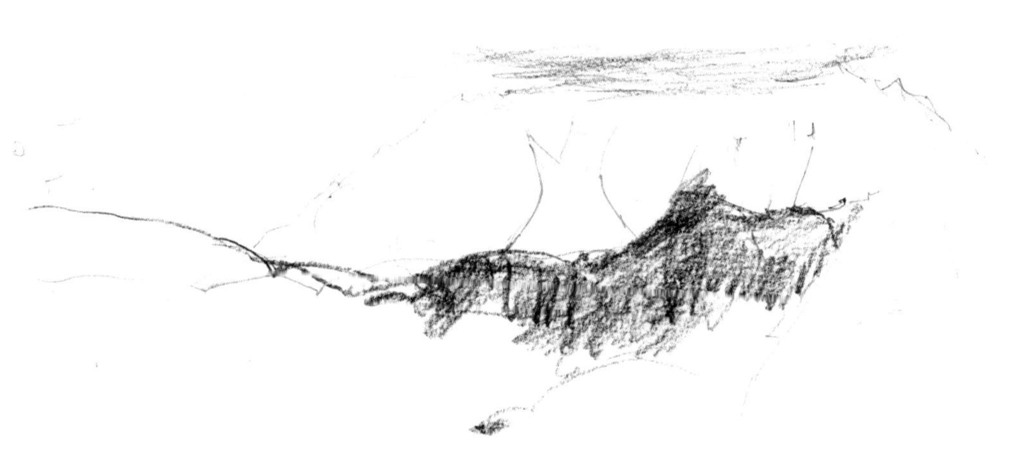

Schneedecke von Zhovkva
2016
15-teilig, gebrannter und glasierter Ton
3 x 155 x 77 cm

snow cover in Zhovkva
2016
15-part piece, fired and glazed clay
3 x 155 x 77 cm

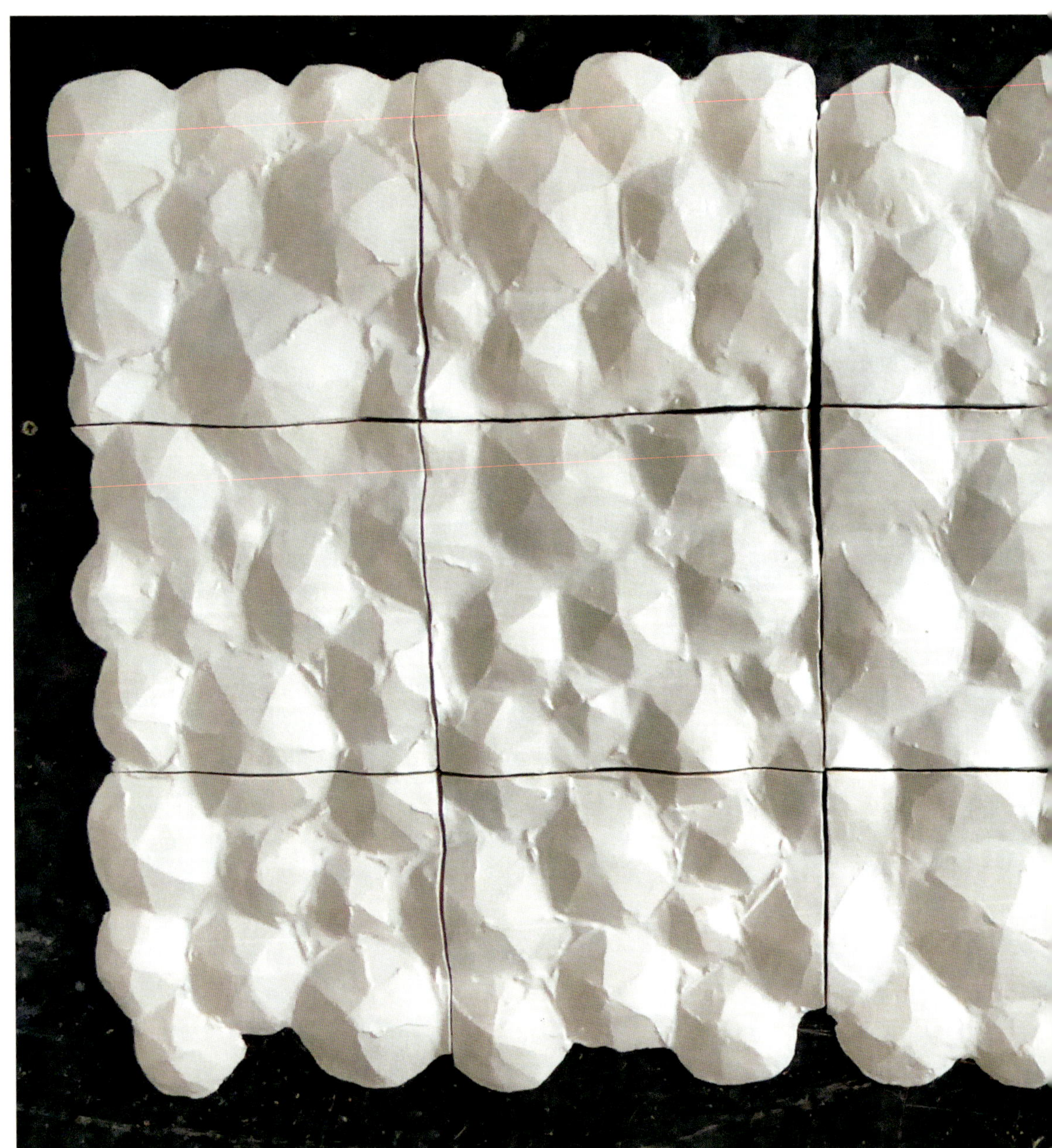

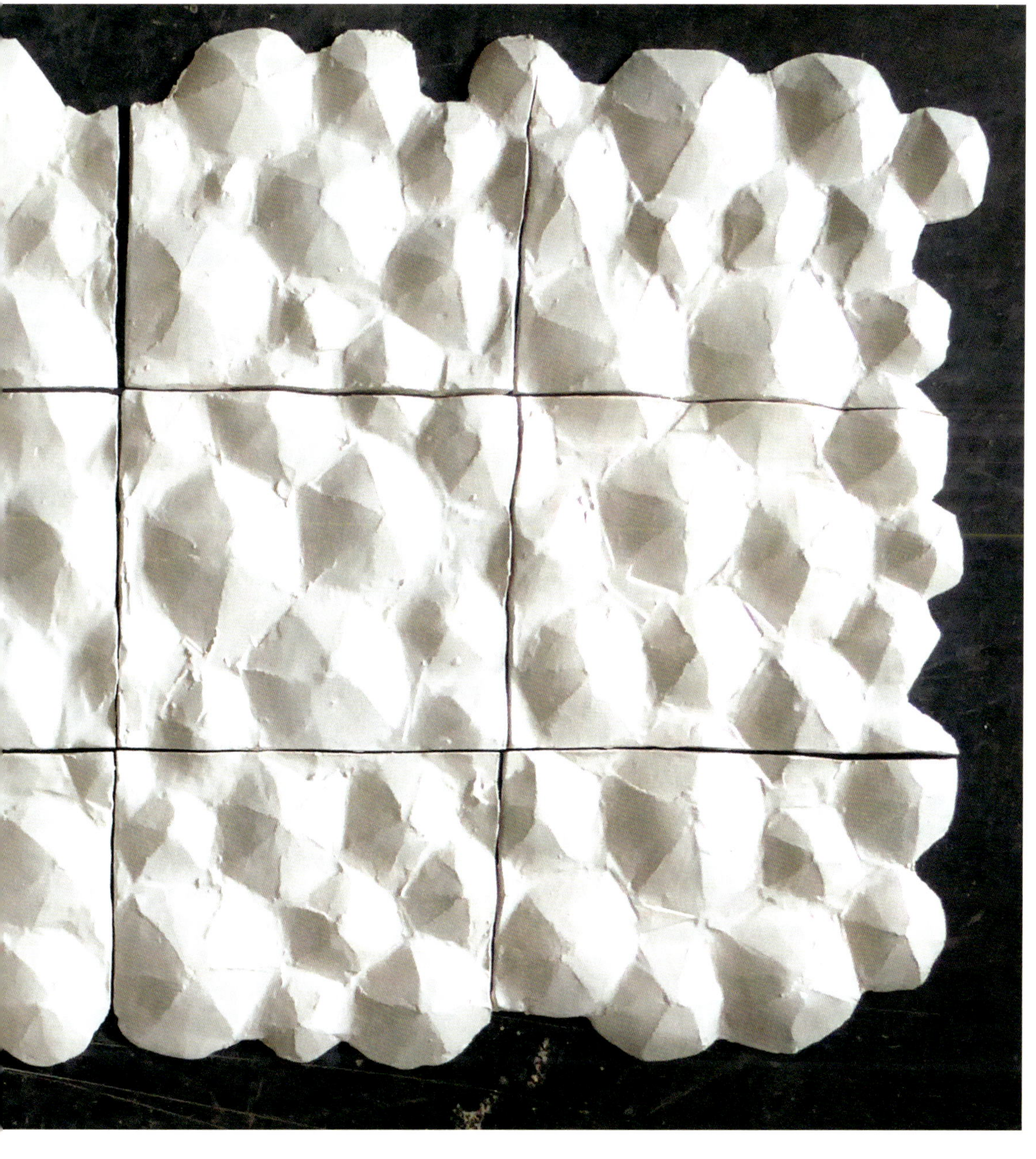

Zicklein im Pamirgebirge
goatling in the Pamir mountains

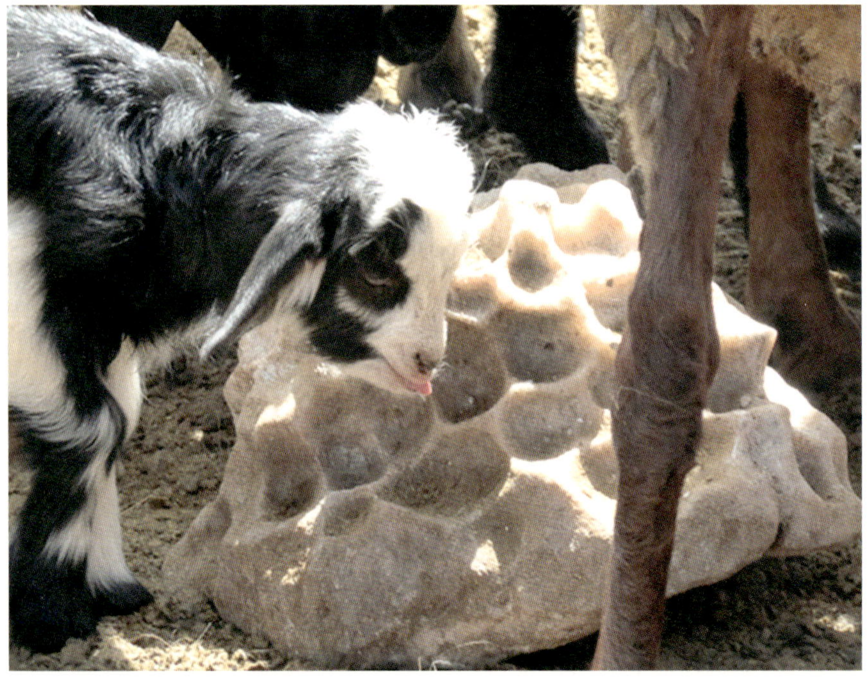

Lecksteine für Caprini
2016
2 Stück, gebrannter und glasierter Ton
5 x 40 x 26 cm, 5 x 36 x 22 cm

leckstones for Caprinae
2016
2 pieces, fired and glazed clay
5 x 40 x 26 cm, 5 x 36 x 22 cm

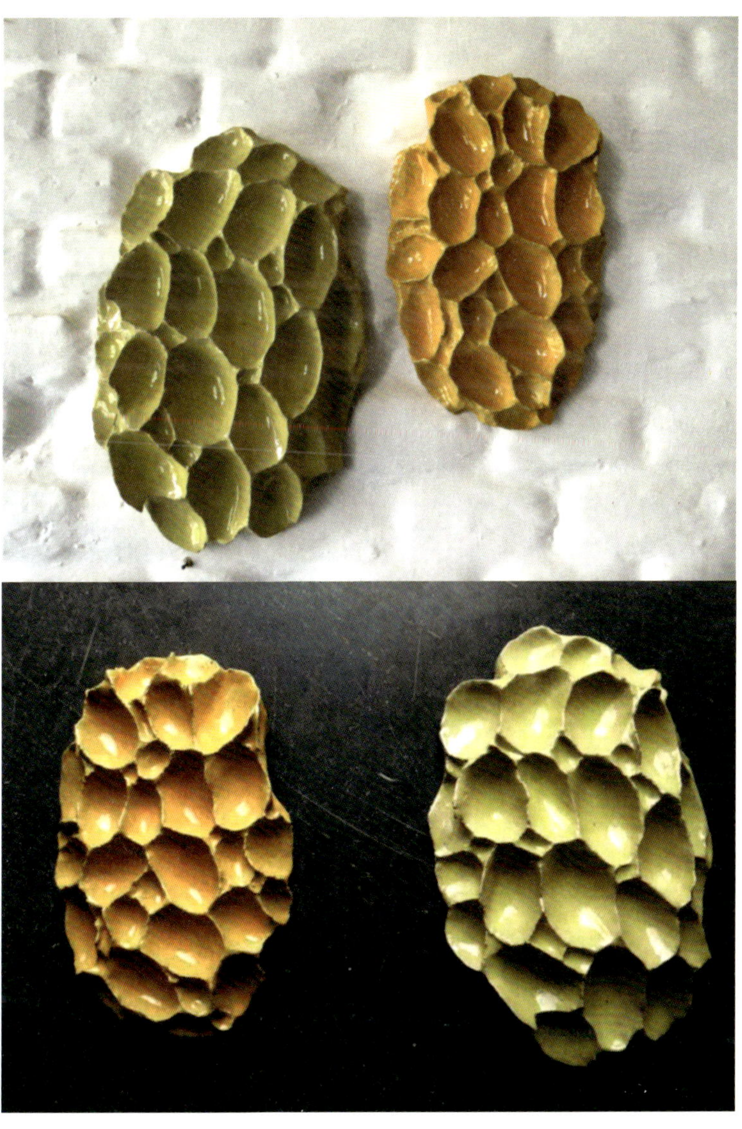

Birne
2016
gebrannter Ton
H 15 cm

pear
2016
fired clay
H 15 cm

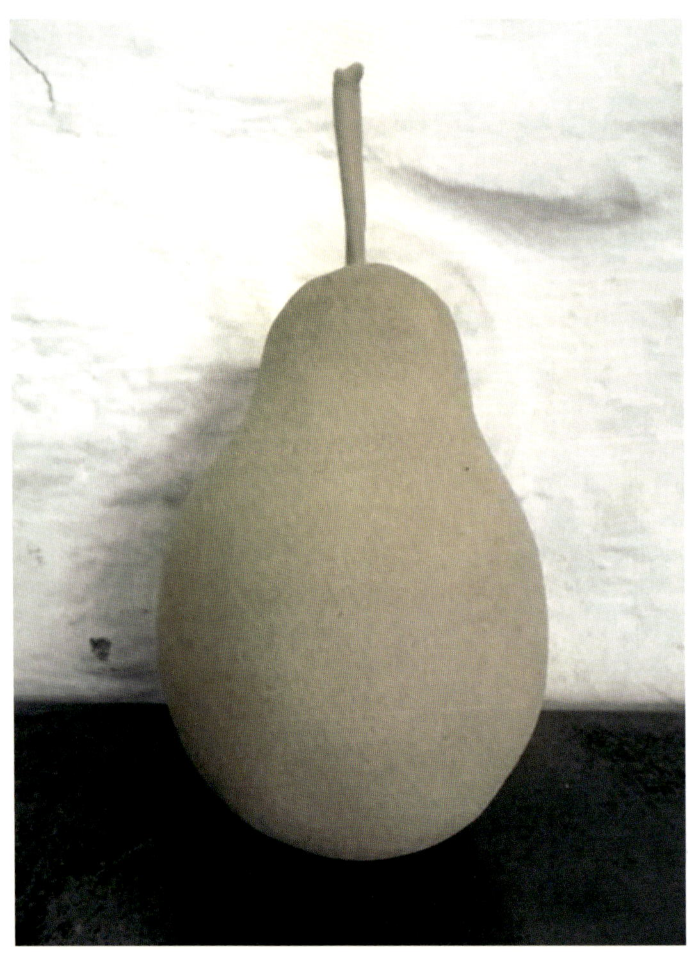

Äpfel
2016
8 Stück, gebrannter Ton
Originalgrößen

apples
2016
8 pieces, fired clay
original sizes

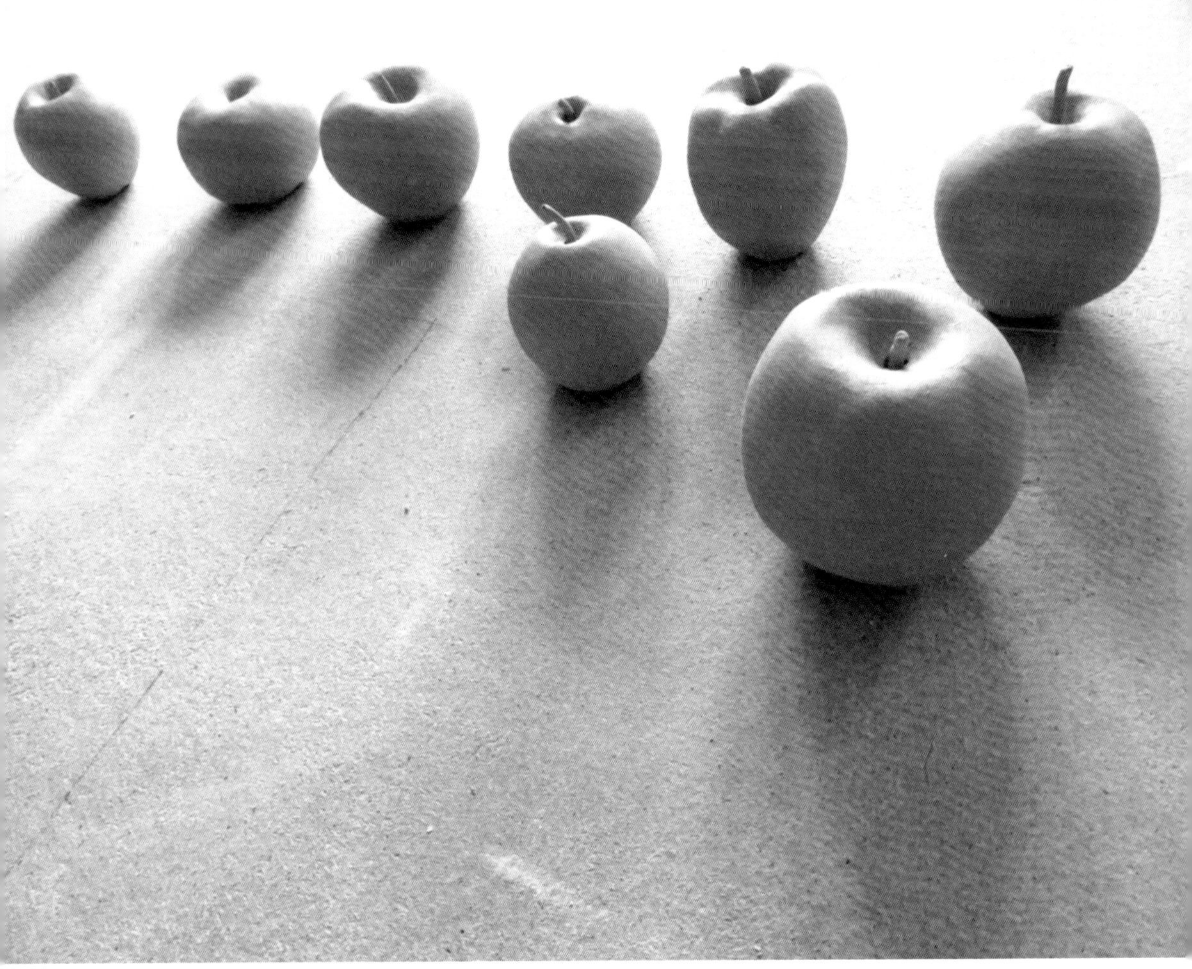

die Ungerösteten
2016
8 Stück, gebrannter und glasierter Ton
à 2 x 17 x 10 cm

the unroasted
2016
8 pieces, fired and glazed clay
2 x 17 x 10 cm each

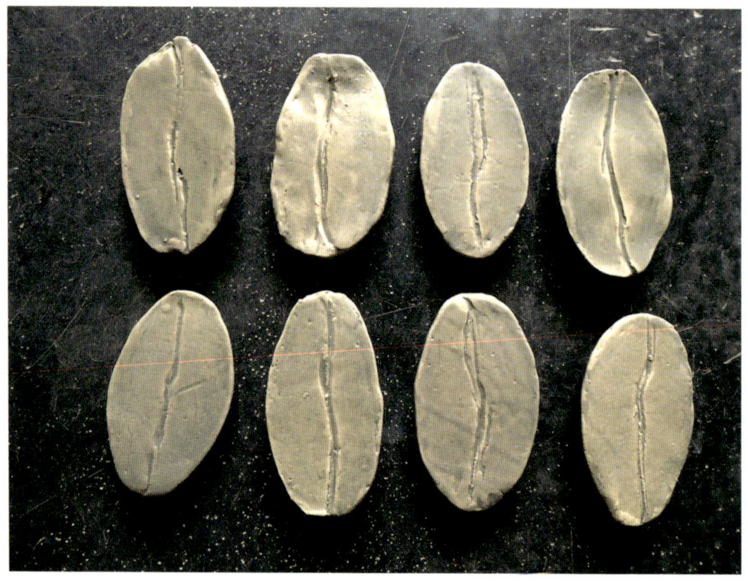

Buddha wirft seinen Schatten
2016
13-teilig, Siebdruck auf gebranntem und glasiertem Ton
Gesamtlänge 5 m

Buddha casts his shadow
2016
13-piece, screenprint on fired and glazed clay
total length 5 m

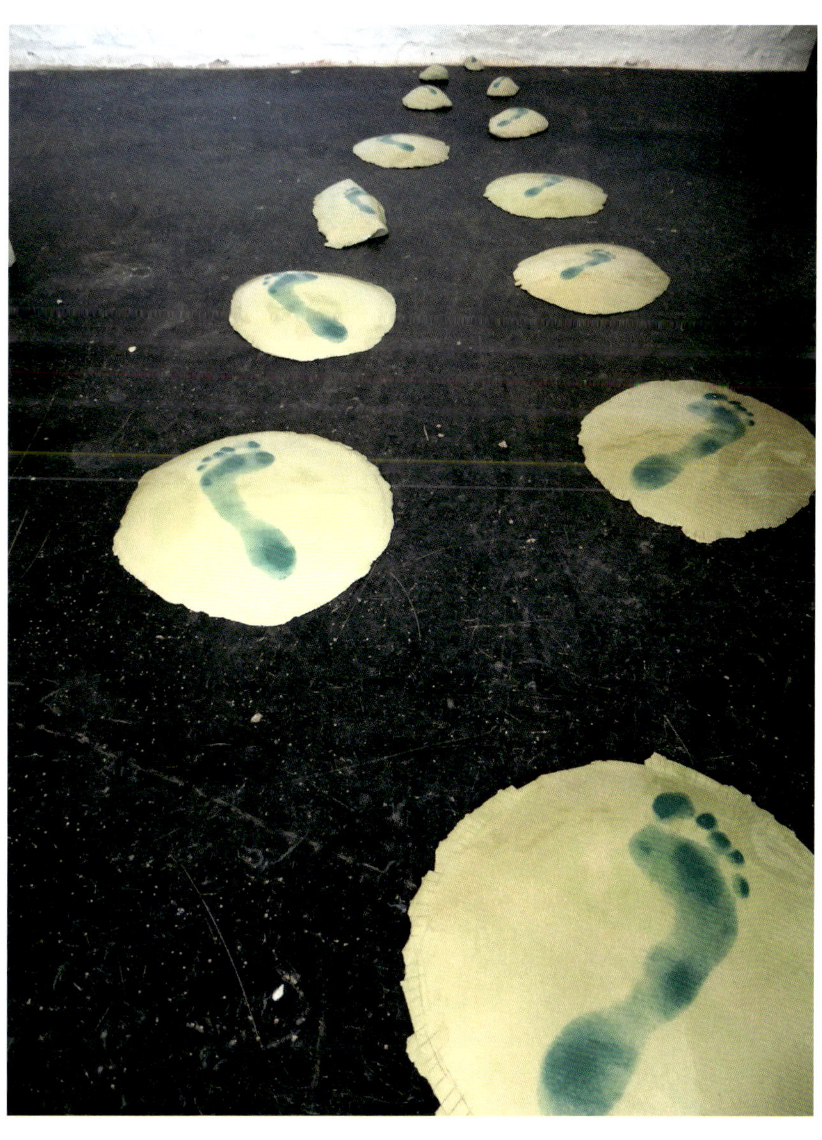

Anna Lorenz

Martina geht auf Reisen

Martina on Tour

„In die gleichen Ströme steigen wir und steigen wir nicht; wir sind es und sind es nicht", sagt Heraklit. Umso mehr gilt das für Reisen. Tag für Tag wirfst du dein Netz aus. Die Quelle hast du im Auge, wenn du suchst. Aus einem Mehr an Bildern schöpfst du, gedreht und gewendet landen sie, sinken sie auf oder unter die Oberfläche. Ohne Zeit und Ort tauchen sie auf, abgenagt manchmal bis auf Form und Struktur. Mit leichtem Gepäck suchst du Stadt und Land auf. Ich habe mich an deine Fersen geheftet und muss dir nur folgen, um zu sehen, wie du suchst und es arbeiten lässt. Wie du dich Schritt um Schritt näherst. Praha oder Lviv in diesem Fall. Wie du dann auch deine Ideen den Elementen aussetzt, dem Wasser und der Erde, der Kälte und der Hitze, den Augen und Händen. Nicht nur den Dingen Freiheit lässt, sich zu entfalten, und dir Freiheit zu entdecken. Die Welt hat sich im Urknall zerstreut und verlorene Dinge wollen eingesammelt werden. „Ein Stein, ein Blatt, eine nichtgefundne Tür; von einem Stein, einem Blatt, einer Tür", schreibt Thomas Wolfe. Als Reisefreundin darf man am Netz aus Worten mitweben und die Landkarte mitschreiben. Das ist mehr als inspirierend. Undramatisch, als wäre es das normalste Schwierige, einen anderen Raum zu betreten. Wenn du alles offen lässt, bleibt auch mir die Freiheit mich zu dehnen, zu drehen und zu wenden. Was dir zufällt und gefällt, wird umwandert, von allen Seiten betrachtet und aufgenommen, als analoges Bild oder als Eindruck. Wenn es geduldig ist, denn du bist geduldig, wird ein flirrender Schwarm auf eine weitere Ebene gehoben, durchgeschleust. In diesem Raum, deinem Kosmos, finden sich Bilder, Worte und Klänge, aus denen du schöpfen kannst. Wenn du reist oder tönerst, gibt es kein Ende, alles fließt über in Anfänge.

"No man ever steps in the same river twice, for it's not the same river and he's not the same man," says Heracleitus. This sentiment is just as cogent when applied to travel. Day after day you throw out your net. You keep your eye on the source as you search. You draw from an abundance of pictures, twisted and turned they land, they drop to or below the surface. Without time or place they appear, sometimes gnawed down to form and structure. Traveling lightly, you visit city and country. I am hard on your heels and need only to follow you to see how you seek and allow it to work. As you approach, getting closer with every step. Prague or Lviv in this case. How you then expose your ideas to the elements, to water and earth, to the cold and the heat, to the eyes and hands. Not only giving the things freedom to unfold, and yourself the freedom to discover. The world has been scattered in the big bang, and lost things long to be collected. "A stone, a leaf, an unfound door; a stone, a leaf, a door," writes Thomas Wolfe. As a travel companion, one is allowed to co-weave the net of words and to help write the map. That is more than inspiring. Undramatic, as if it were the most normal difficult thing, to enter another room. If you leave everything open, the freedom is there for me to stretch myself and to twist and turn. What comes to you and pleases you is circumnavigated, considered from all sides and taken in, as an analog image or as an impression. If it is patient, because you are patient, a flickering shoal is raised to another level, guided through. In this room, your cosmos, there are pictures, words, and sounds, from which you can draw. When you travel or make pottery, there is no end; everything overflows into beginnings.

Detail aus **Buddha wirft seinen Schatten** (S. 93)
Detail from **Buddha casts his shadow** (p. 93)

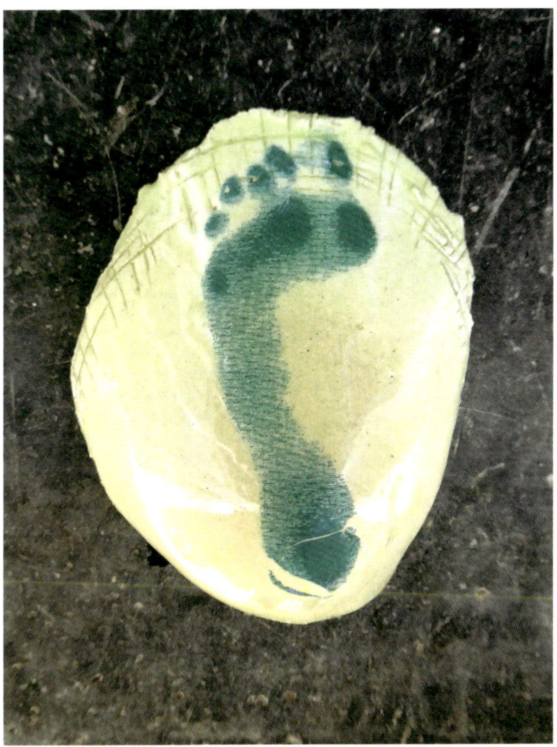

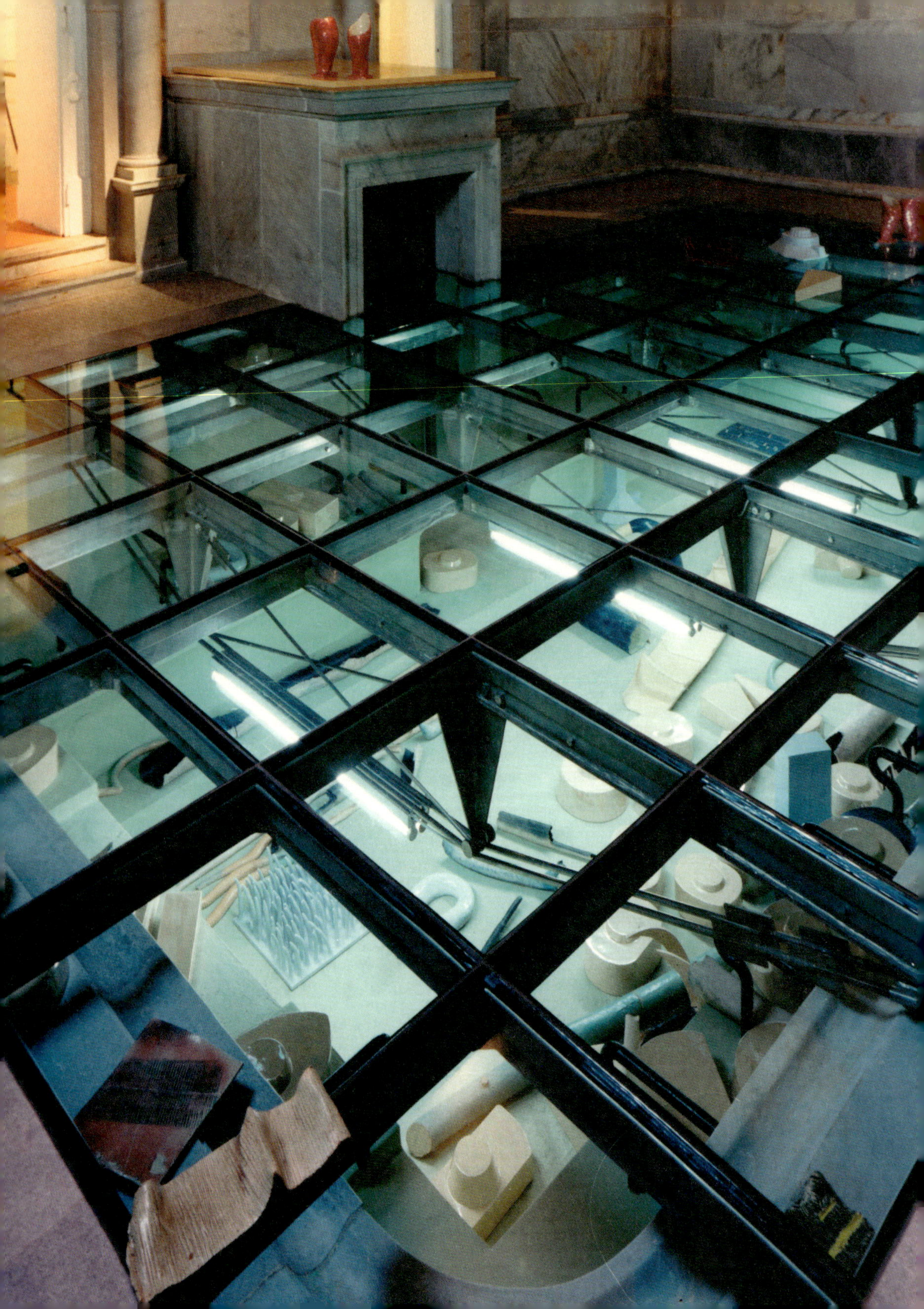

Biographie Biography
Martina Funder

1953 geboren in Wien born in Vienna
1973–1978 Akademie der bildenden Künste Wien, Meisterklasse für Malerei Academy of Fine Arts Vienna, master class in painting
1978 Diplom Diplom
1981–1985 Hochschule für künstlerische und industrielle Gestaltung Linz, Meisterklasse für Keramik University of Art and Industrial Design in Linz, Austria, master class in ceramics
1985 Diplom Diplom
seit since 1979 Mitglied des Kunstvereins Baden Member of the Baden Art Association
seit since 1985 freiberuflich in Baden bei Wien tätig Freelance work in Baden, Austria
1996–2000 Obfrau des Kunstvereins Baden

Auswahl von Einzelausstellungen (EA) und Teilnahme an Gruppenausstellungen Selected solo exhibitions (SE) and participation in group exhibitions

2016 Kulturwerkstatt10, Fürstenfeldbruck, DE
2015/16 *5th Biennal Exhibition of drawings Serbia,* Belgrad, Novi Sad, RS
100 Meisterwerke, Kunstverein Baden
Dis/Order. Vom Wesen dynamischer Systeme, Kunst im öffentlichen Raum, 100 Jahre KV Baden (Katalog catalog)
Salzburger Keramikpreis, Galerie im Traklhaus, Salzburg (Katalog catalog)
2014 *235 km/100 years Part of Danube Dialogues,* Contemporary Gallery Zrenjanin, RS
Sensing the mind-Minding the sense, Kunstverein Baden
2010 *Salzburger Keramikpreis,* Galerie im Traklhaus, Salzburg, Gmunden, Heiligenkreuzerhof Wien (Katalog catalog)
to connect, Haus der Kunst, Baden (EA SE)
2008 Kunsthalle Tatabánya, HU Gallery of Contemporary Art Tatabánya, Hungary (Katalog catalog)
2007 *Off and go,* Kunstverein Baden
2002 *Linzer Augen,* OÖ. Kunstverein, Ursulinenhof, Linz
looking over the border, Kunsthalle Szombathely, HU Gallery of Szombathely, HU (Katalog catalog)
2000 *Kunstverein Baden,* Wrocław, PL
1999 *Kunstverein Baden,* Kölner Kunstverein, Köln, DE
233 m über dem Meeresspiegel, Kunstverein Bozenn
Bestandsaufnahme, Kammerhofgalerie, Gmunden (EA SE)
1996 *Badewetter,* Kunsthaus Frauenbad, Baden
Keramik-Skulptur, Körper-Volumen, Hipphalle Gmunden (Katalog catalog)
Lichtwege, Weihnachtsbeleuchtung Wassergasse Baden (Katalog catalog)
1995 *Donald Judd and artist friends,* Galerie nächst St. Stephan, Wien
1994 *2. Internationale Keramikbiennale Kairo,* Kairo Cairo, EG (Katalog catalog)
1992 *Kleine Skulpturen,* Galerie Menotti, Baden
1991 *Neue österreichische Keramik,* Galerie an der Stadtmauer, Villach (Katalog catalog)
Configura, Erfurt, DE (Katalog catalog)
Ceramic Arts gallery, Wien (EA SE)
1990 DOK St. Pölten (EA SE)
Plastik, Gefäss und Entwurf, Galerie auf der Stubenbastei, Wien
1. Internationales Seminar, Gaia, PTI (Katalog catalog)
Zeitgenössische Keramik aus Österreich, Keramion Museum, Frechen, DE (Katalog catalog)
Eröffnungsausstellung der Galerie ceramic arts opening exhibition of the Galerie ceramic arts, Wien
1989 *L'Europe des ceramistes,* Auxerre, FR, Wanderausstellung durch Europa traveling exhibition through Europe (Katalog catalog)
Konfrontationen, Messepalast, Wien (Katalog catalog)
1988 *De clii Galerie,* Glarus, CH
1987 *4 x 1,* Künstlerhaus Palais Thurn und Taxis, Bregenz
1986 *Kunstformen jetzt,* Salzburg
Art Gallery, Keramikstudio Krugerstraße, Wien
Österreichisches Kulturinstitut Austrian Cultural Forum, New York, USA
1985 *Romulus Express,* Künstlerhaus Klagenfurt, Galerie Insam, Wien (Katalog catalog)
1984 *12 Keramikerinnen aus Österreich,* Galerie Ludwig, Hannover, DE (Katalog catalog)
1983 *3. Römerquellewettbewerb,* Galerie auf der Stubenbastei, Stadthaus Klagenfurt, Neue Galerie der Stadt Linz (Katalog catalog)
Österreichisches Kulturinstitut Austrian Cultural Forum, Kairo Cairo, EG (EA SE)
1982 Wraxhall Gallery, London, GB (EA SE)
Galerie an der Stadtmauer, Villach (Katalog catalog) (EA SE)
1981 Künstlerhaus Palais Thurn und Taxis, Bregenz
1980 *65 Jahre Kunstverein Baden,* Kunsthaus Frauenbad, Baden (Katalog catalog)
Galerie Zweymüller, Baden (EA SE)
17. Österreichische Graphikwettbewerb Innsbruck, Wanderausstellung traveling exhibition (Katalog catalog)
Österreichische Keramik 1900–1980, Wanderausstellung traveling exhibition (Katalog catalog)
Kleine Galerie, Künstlerhaus Klagenfurt (Katalog catalog) (EA SE)
1979 *16. Österreichische Graphikwettbewerb, Innsbruck,* Wanderausstellung (Katalog catalog)
1978 Galerie Würthle, Wien
1976 Galerie Maier, Innsbruck (EA SE)

Preise u. a. Awards et al.

2005 Einladung zum internationalen Workshop in Yeoju, RK (Katalog catalog)
1993 Salzburger Keramikpreis, Preis des BM für Unterricht und Kunst (Katalog catalog)
1992 Kulturpreis der Stadt Baden
1991 Anerkennungspreis des Landes NÖ (Katalog catalog)

Ausstellung Exhibition ***Badewetter,*** 1996
Kunsthaus Frauenbad, Baden bei Wien

Kachelofen *Vinschgauer*
2002
Tschars, Südtirol

tiled stove *Vinschgau*
2002
Tschars, Southern Tyrol

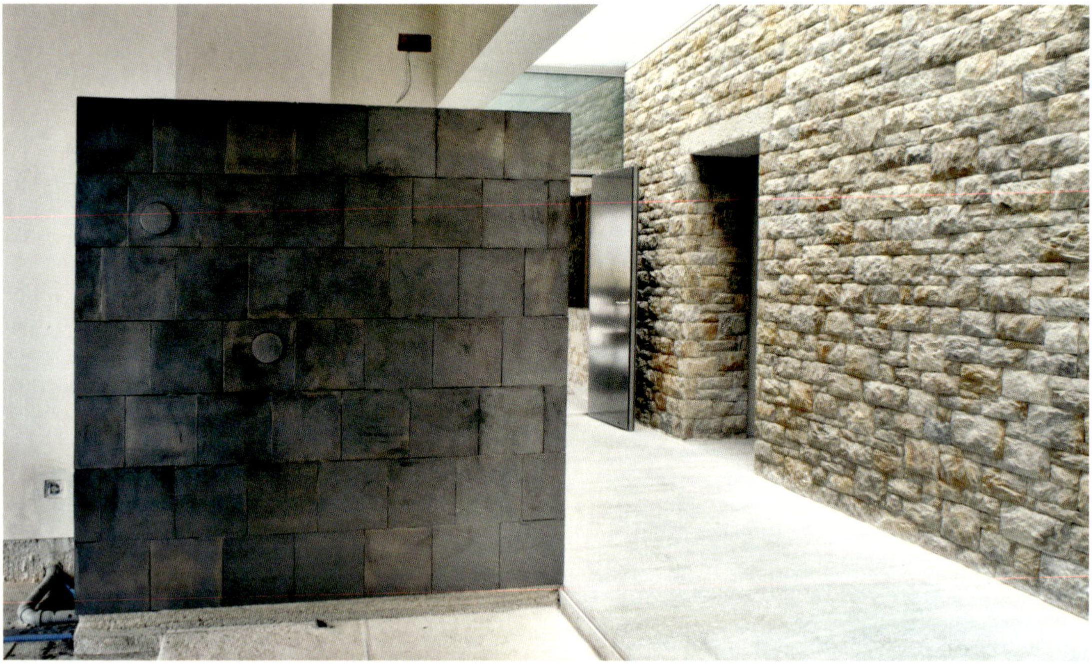

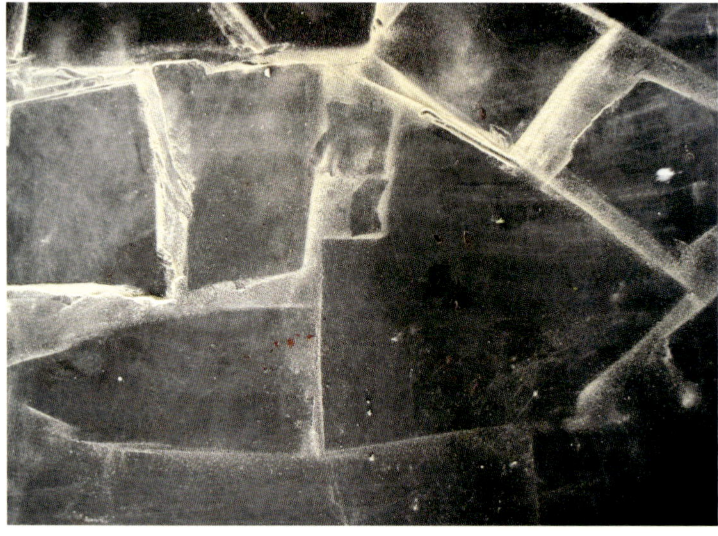

Fußboden der Werkstatt, Baden
Floor of studio, Baden

Ausstellung Exhibition, 1990
NÖ Dokumentationszentrum für moderne Kunst, St. Pölten

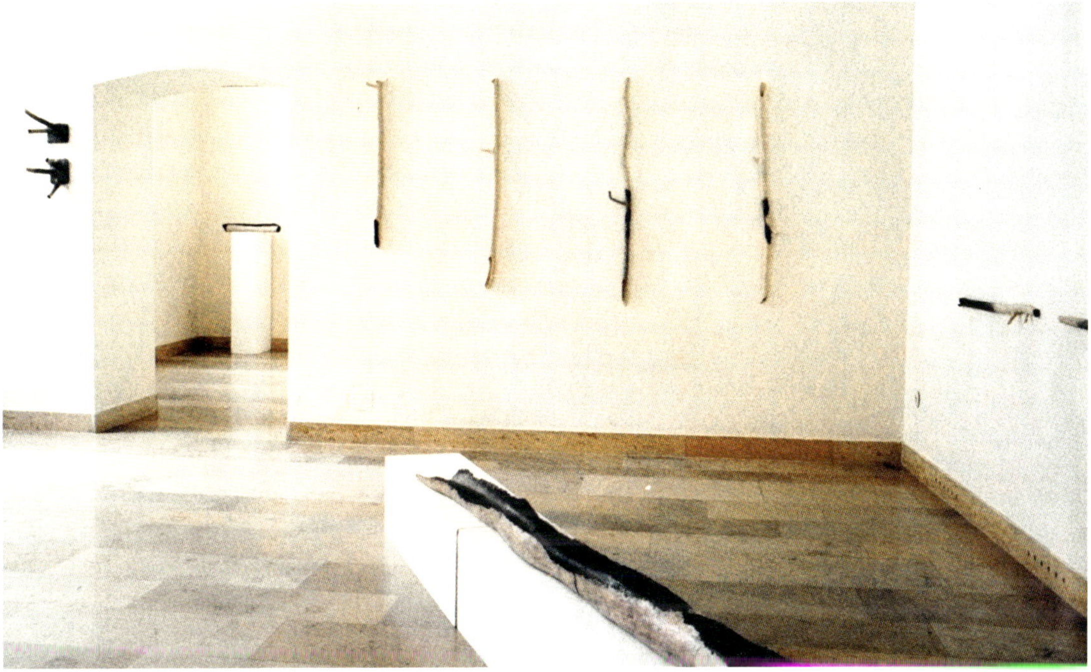

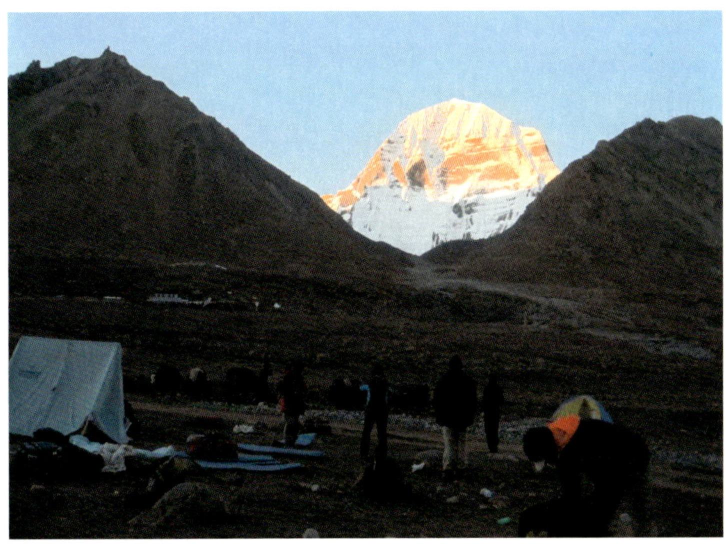

Kailash bei Sonnenaufgang, Tibet
Kailash at sunrise, Tibet

rosa Regal
2015
Metallregal, Keramik, Plexiglas

the pink cabinet
2015
metal shelving, ceramics, plexiglass

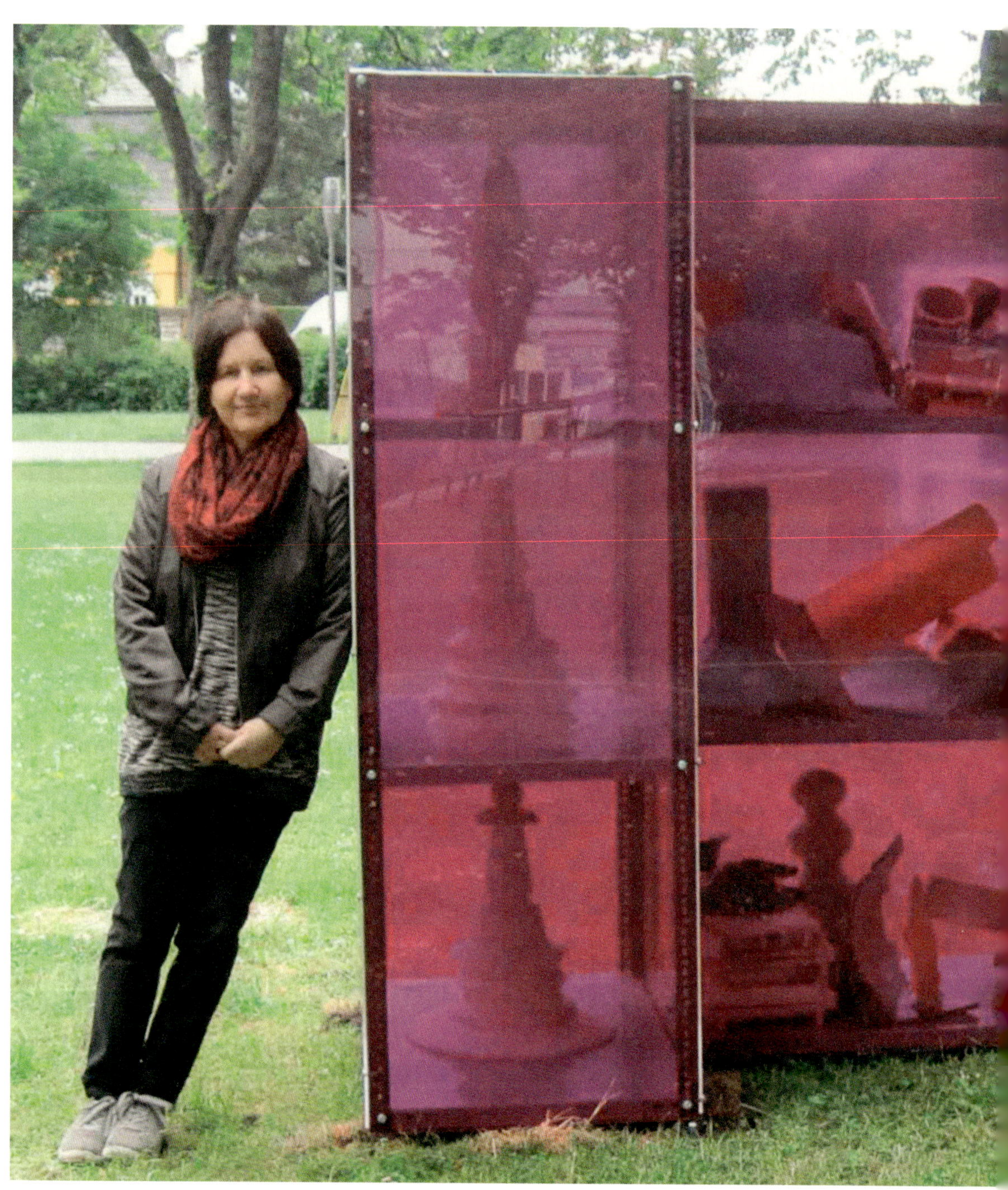

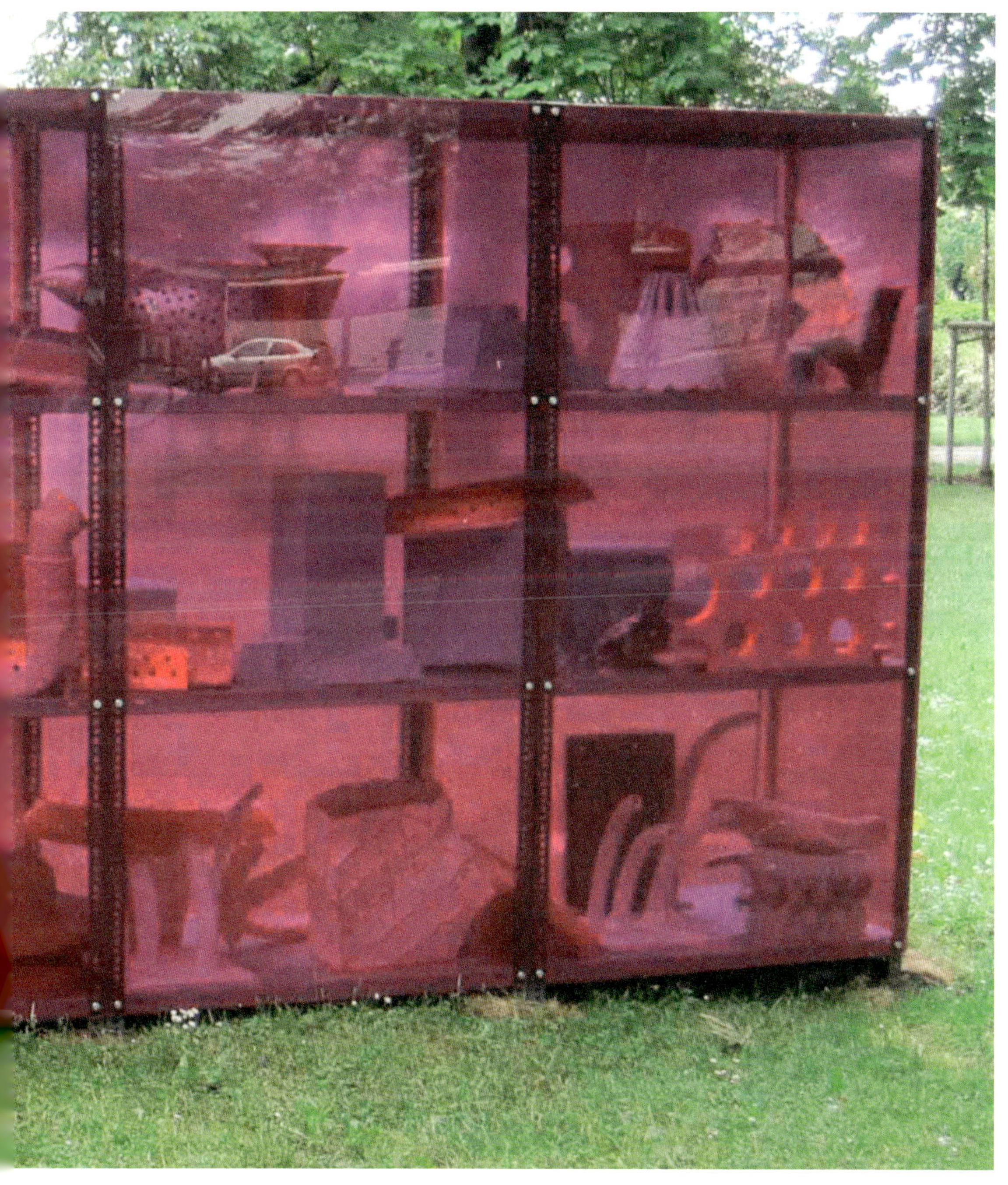

Autor_innen Authors

Rainald Franz
Kunsthistoriker. 1964 geboren in Graz. Studium in Wien, München, London, Rom, Venedig. Seit 1992 im MAK; 1996–2011 Stellvertretender Leiter der Bibliothek und Kunstblättersammlung des MAK – Österreichischen Museums für angewandte Kunst/Gegenwartskunst, ab 2000 Provenienzbeauftragter im MAK, seit Oktober 2011 Leiter der Sammlung Glas und Porzellan sowie zuständig für sammlungsübergreifende und EU-Projekte im MAK. Zahlreiche Ausstellungen und Publikationen, Veranstalter von Symposien, etwa „Gottfried Semper und Wien", zuletzt „Leben mit Loos", Wien 2008. Beteiligung an internationalen Symposien. Lehrbeauftragter am Kunsthistorischen Institut der Universität Wien und am Institut für Konservierung und Restaurierwissenschaften der Universität für angewandte Kunst, Wien: Geschichte der Ornamentik. 2007–2013 Präsident der ICDAD-International Committee of Decorative Arts and Design, 2011–2013 Vorsitzender des Verbandes Österreichischer Kunsthistorikerinnen und Kunsthistoriker. Forschungsschwerpunkte: Architektur der Neuzeit, Geschichte der Ornamentik, des Kunstgewerbes und des frühen Designs.
Art historian. Born 1964 in Graz, Austria. Studied in Vienna, Munich, London, Rome, and Venice. As of 1992, held various positions at the MAK (Austrian Museum of Applied Arts/Contemporary Art): 1996–2011 Deputy head of the library and art collection; from 2000 Provenance representative; from October 2011 Head of the collection of glass and ceramics, as well as responsible for cross-collection projects and EU projects. Numerous exhibitions and publications, symposia organization, such as *Gottfried Semper und Wien* (Gottfried Semper and Vienna), and the recent *Leben mit Loos* (Live with Loos), Vienna 2008. Participation in international symposia. Lecturer at the Institute of Art History, University of Vienna and the Institute for Conservation and Restoration Science of the University of Applied Arts Vienna: history of ornamentation. 2007–2013 President of ICDAD – International Committee of Decorative Arts and Design. 2011–2013 Chairman of the Association of Austrian Art Historians. Research focal points: contemporary architecture, history of ornamentation, of the applied arts/decorative art, and of early design.

Renée Gadsden
Autorin, Kunst- und Kulturhistorikerin. Dr. phil. der Kultur- und Geistesgeschichte, Universität für angewandte Kunst Wien (2002). Mag. art. in Bildhauerei (Klasse Brigitte Kowanz), Universität für angewandte Kunst Wien (1999). Artium Baccalaureus der Kunst und Kunstgeschichte, Brown University, Providence, Rhode Island (1985). Mitbegründerin (zusammen mit Christian Ide Hintze, Gert Jonke u. a.) und stellvertretende Vorstandsvorsitzende des Komitees „Akademie für Sprachkunst", um Creative Writing in Österreich auf Hochschulebene unterrichten zu lassen. Consultant und Manager für Kunst, Kultur und Bildung, Wien und New York (seit 1994). Universitätsdozentin, Abteilung für Kunsttheorie am Institut für Arts and Science, Universität für Angewandte Kunst Wien (seit 2013). Universitätsdozentin der Staffordshire University an der Werbe Akademie Wien, Bachelor of Arts in Grafikdesign, Werbung und Programm für Markenmanagement (2012/2013). Projektleiterin und -koordinatorin, Knowledge Art Space, KMA – Knowledge Management Austria (2009/2010). Universitätsassistentin der Abteilung Kultur- und Geistesgeschichte, Universität für angewandte Kunst Wien (2002–2006). Kulturredakteurin und Radioshowmoderatorin, ORF Wien (2000–2002). Kunstvermittlerin der Bildungsabteilung, Museum Moderner Kunst Stiftung Ludwig Wien (1994–2000). Leiterin der Abteilung Bildung und Vermittlung des Kulturprogramms der Arbeiterkammer Wien (1994 – 2000). Managing Director, One World Agency für PR, Marketing und Veranstaltung Wien (1995–1998).
Author, art historian and cultural historian. Dr. phil. in Cultural and Intellectual History, University of Applied Arts Vienna (2002). M.A. in Sculpture (under B. Kowanz), University of Applied Arts, Vienna (1999). B.A. in Art and Art History, Brown University, Providence, Rhode Island (1985). Co-founder (together with Christian Ide Hintze, Gert Jonke et al.) and deputy chairperson of the "Akademie für Sprachkunst" (Academy for Language Arts) committee, for teaching university-level creative writing in Austria. Consultant and manager for art, culture and education, Vienna and New York (since 1994). University lecturer, Department of Art Theory at the Institute for Arts and Science, University of Applied Arts Vienna (since 2013). University lecturer of Staffordshire University at the Werbe Akademie Wien (Advertising Academy Vienna), B.A. in Graphic Design, Advertising and Program for Brand Management (2012/2013). Project manager and coordinator, Knowledge Art Space, KMA – Knowledge Management Austria (2009–2010). Assistant Professor of the Department of Cultural and Intellectual History, University of Applied Arts Vienna (2002–2006). Cultural editor and radio show host, ORF Vienna (2000 – 2002). Art mediator in the Department of Education, Museum of Modern Art Ludwig Foundation Vienna (February 1994–2000). Education and Cultural Program Communication Dept. Head for the Vienna Chamber of Labor (1994. 2000). Managing director, One World Agency für PR, Marketing und Veranstaltung (PR, Marketing and Event Management), Vienna (1995–1998).

Hartwig Knack
Kunstwissenschaftler, Kurator und Autor. 1964 geboren in Kamen, Deutschland. Studium der Kunstgeschichte, Kunst, Europäischen Ethnologie und der Kulturwissenschaften an den Universitäten Marburg an der Lahn und Wien sowie des Museums- und Ausstellungswesens am Institut für Kulturwissenschaft Wien. Edgar Ende-Stiftung München & Frankfurt am Main (1994–2000). Künstlerischer Leiter der Factory Krems; Leitung des internationalen Artist-in-Residence-Programms der Abteilung Kultur und Wissenschaft des Landes Niederösterreich (2002–2009). Kurator der Kunsthalle Krems (2003–2009). Arbeit als freier Kunstwissenschaftler, Kurator und Autor (seit 2010). Zahlreiche Publikationen im Bereich der Kunst und Kulturgeschichte (Auswahl): *K.U.SCH. Renate Krätschmer und Jörg Schwarzenberger,* Zeit.Kunst Niederösterreich, hg. v. Alexandra Schantl, Kerber Verlag, Bielefeld 2014; *4muerz2beat14 – für Mürzzuschlag 14,* Kunsthaus Muerz, Steinverlag, Bad Traunstein 2014; *Das neue Stadtpalais Prinz Eugen. Ein Dialog zwischen kulturellem Erbe und moderner Architektur,* hg. gem. mit Heinrich Strixner, Brandstätter Verlag, Wien 2014.
Art historian, curator and author. Born in Kamen, Germany 1964. Studied Art History, Art, European Ethnology and Cultural Studies at the Universities of Marburg and Vienna, as well as Museum and Exhibition Management at the Institute of Cultural Studies Vienna. Edgar Ende Foundation, Munich and Frankfurt am Main (1994–2000). Artistic Director of Factory Krems; Direction of the international Artist-in-Residence Program of the Department of Culture and Science of Lower Austria (2002–2009). Curator, Kunsthalle Krems (2003–2009). Freelance art historian, curator and author (since 2010). Numerous publications in the field of art and cultural history. Selection: *K.U.SCH. Renate Krätschmer and Jörg Schwarzenberger,* Zeit.Kunst. Lower Austria, edited by Alexandra Schantl, published by Kerber Verlag, Bielefeld 2014. *4muerz2beat14 – für Mürzzuschlag 14,* Kunsthaus Muerz, published by Stein Verlag, Bad Traunstein 2014. *Das neue Stadtpalais Prinz Eugen. Ein Dialog zwischen kulturellem Erbe und moderner Architektur,* released with Heinrich Strixner, published by Brandstätter Verlag, Vienna 2014.

Anna Lorenz

Geboren 1959 in Wien, Studium der Judaistik und Arabistik an der Universität Wien, arbeitet fur diverse Verlage.

Born in Vienna 1959, studied Judaism and Arabism at the University of Vienna, works for several publishing houses.

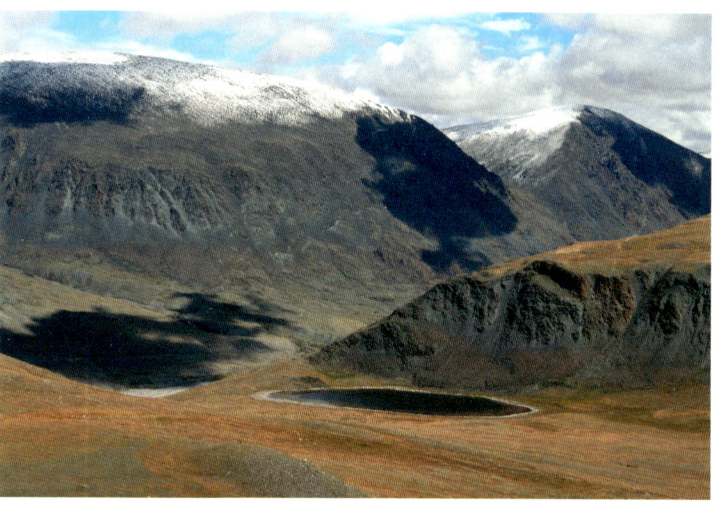

Berg der Steinböcke, Altaigebirge, Mongolei
mountain of ibexes, mountains of Altai, Mongolia

Impressum Colophon

Texte Essays: Rainald Franz, Renée Gadsden, Hartwig Knack, Anna Lorenz
Grafikdesign Graphic design: Maria Anna Friedl
Lithografie Lithography: Pixelstorm, Wien Vienna
Lektorat Copy-editing: Anna Mirfattahi
Übersetzung Translations: Jennifer Weidenholzer, Renée Gadsen (S. p. 45)
Typografie Typography: Univers
Papier Paper: GardaPat 13 KIARA
Druck und Bindung Printing and binding: Remaprint Litteradruck, Wien Vienna

Erschienen im Published by

Mit besonderem Dank an Anna Lorenz, ohne sie wäre das Buch nie zustande gekommen.
With special thanks to Anna Lorenz, without her this book would have never been possible.

VfmK Verlag für moderne Kunst GmbH
Salmgasse 4a, A-1030 Wien
T: +43-(0)1-5354970-15
www.vfmk.org
hello@vfmk.org

ISBN 9783903131651

Die Deutsche Nationalbibliothek verzeichnet diese Publikation in der Deutschen Nationalbibliografie; detaillierte bibliografische Daten sind im Internet über http://dnb.ddb.de abrufbar.
The Deutsche Nationalbibliothek lists this publication in the Deutsche Nationalbibliografie; detailed bibliographic data is available on the internet at http://dnb.ddb.de.

Vertrieb Distribution
D, A und Europa and Europe: LKG, www.lkg-va.de
CH: AVA, www.ava.ch
UK: Cornerhouse Publications, www.cornerhousepublications.org
USA: D.A.P., www.artbook.com

Bildnachweis Picture credits

© Thomas Kaminski: S. pp. 10–15, 18–25, 30/31, 33, 37, 39, 67, 68–71
© Gabi Lohinger: S. pp. 100/101
© Arch. Elisabeth Schatzer: S. p. 98
© Martina Funder: alle anderen Fotos all other photos